ABSTINENCE IN ACTION

♦ ♦ ♦

ABSTINENCE IN ACTION

• • •

Food Planning for Compulsive Eaters

Barbara McFarland, Ed.D.
Anne Marie Erb, M.Ed., R.D.

1817

A Hazelden Book

Harper & Row, Publishers, San Francisco

New York, Grand Rapids, Philadelphia, St. Louis
London, Singapore, Sydney, Tokyo, Toronto

FIRST HARPER & ROW EDITION PUBLISHED IN 1990.

Library of Congress Cataloging-in-Publication Data

McFarland, Barbara.
    Abstinence in action : food planning for compulsive eaters / Barbara McFarland, Anne Marie Erb.
      p.   cm.
    Includes bibliographical references.
    ISBN 0-06-255379-8 :
    1. Compulsive eating.   I. Erb, Anne Marie. II. Title.
RC552.C65M249 1990
616.85'260654—dc20   90-30304
                                                              CIP

LC 87-45189
ISBN 0-06-255379-8

---

90 91 92 93 94   10 9 8 7 6 5 4 3 2 1

Contents

Preface

I first came to treat alcoholics as a part of my clinical training as a psychologist in 1977. My original goal was to receive the supervision required for licensure and then to begin a private practice. These plans changed within a few months of my internship. I found my work with chemically dependent patients to be the most rewarding and challenging clinical experience. My interest expanded to the clinical treatment of alcoholic women since I felt the treatment program primarily addressed the male issues of the disease. It was through my work with alcoholic women that I became aware of and interested in food addiction.

Since 1980, I have worked with hundreds of women and men who feel totally out of control when it comes to eating. Many of these compulsive eaters are adult children of alcoholics, drug dependent themselves, or are married to someone chemically dependent. They report feeling great shame over a compulsion they think should be under their control. Often, when I compare compulsive eating to alcoholism, I hear a deep sigh of relief: "Yes! That is exactly how I feel. Like an alcoholic, only with food."

Many of these people report that they eat especially in times of stress. This stress is often related to anxiety which is the result of unexpressed needs and feelings. Just like the alcoholic who can't stop at one drink, the compulsive eater continues to binge. One cookie is never enough.

There are people who occasionally abuse food or alcohol, but their lives are not out of control. The compulsive eater and alcoholic are obsessed with their addictions to the point that they develop behaviors to protect the use of their substance.

Denial is a powerful part of the addictive process. The ever-present belief system that says, "I am not a compulsive eater, I can control my eating" keeps the disease active. For compulsive eaters, "control" is supported by the wider culture in the form of fad diets. There are ads on television, billboards, and in magazines that promote diets, pills, and workout programs. Many compulsive eaters are deluded into believing they can buy control.

Compulsive eating can be a devastating illness. It has taken a long time to accept alcoholism as a disease and not view it as a weakness of will. We are only beginning to understand the compulsive eater. The fat person, the vomiter or laxative abuser, is often viewed as someone who is disgusting and out of control.

In 1984 I opened the Eating Disorders Recovery Center in Cincinnati, Ohio — an outpatient comprehensive treatment center. I developed the program with the philosophy that compulsive eating is a chronic, progressive disease similar to alcoholism. I believe compulsive eating requires intensive treatment that should include group and individual therapy, educational lectures, a strong family program, nutrition education, and body image groups (people in these groups focus on their perceptions of their body size, and they learn to be more realistic in accepting their bodies).

Two key elements in early recovery from the disease include *a sound abstinence concept* and *a comprehensive food and exercise plan.* Abstinence is a different issue for compulsive eaters than it is for chemically dependent people. A person cannot abstain from food. Abstinence from compulsive eating has three main components: physical abstinence, emotional abstinence, and spiritual abstinence. *Physical abstinence* means abstaining from dieting and rigid, excessive eating or exercise habits. *Emotional abstinence* is abstaining from negative, self-defeating thinking and behavior. By *spiritual abstinence,* I mean abstaining from the belief that *I am alone in the world.*

This book is part of the Eating Disorders Recovery Center food and exercise planning program. This program, which integrates the abstinence concept, has worked for our patients and it can work for you. *Abstinence in Action: Food Planning for Compulsive Eaters* is not a diet book; this is a guide to developing an individual food and exercise plan for compulsive eaters. We will further explore our abstinence model and strategies for developing your own food and exercise planning activities.

Our primary mission is to help you abandon the merry-go-round of dieting. A diet to a compulsive eater is like a drink to the alcoholic. Compulsive eating needs to be treated in a comprehensive manner, not just by dieting alone. Diets often keep compulsive eaters "drunk" on the idea that there is a quick fix diet that will transform them.

Abstinence in Action is intended to help you learn about your eating patterns and to assist you in developing a sound abstinence concept that can be integrated into your food and exercise plan.

Barbara McFarland, Ed.D.
Psychologist

Introduction

As many of us know, compulsive eating is a torturous way of life. We may spend hours thinking and worrying about:

- what we should or should not eat;
- how much we should or should not eat; and
- when and if we should or should not eat.

For some of us, these thoughts occupy our minds, control our activities, and create feelings of guilt, anger, self-hate, and resentment.

Food takes on enormous power in our lives when it's used to cope with stress and painful feelings. In this way food is used as a drug, helping to temporarily reduce the anxiety that bad feelings create. For some of us, food is a way to meet emotional needs. The hunger goes beyond the physical; there is a deep-felt emptiness within that we try desperately to fill up.

False relief often comes in the guise of a diet or purge, such as vomiting, frantic exercise, laxative abuse, or fasting. Initially, these activities may help us feel more in control; in reality, dieting or purging bring more havoc to our lives.

Research indicates that dieting often incites an eating disorder. It fuels compulsive eating by creating an atmosphere of strict deprivation that is impossible to maintain. It also alters the metabolism. When we diet extensively, our metabolism quickly adjusts by slowing down to compensate for less food. This results in a dramatic slowdown of weight loss and often brings it to a halt.

Many of us probably begin every new diet with a great sense of relief and motivation. *This will be the one! This one will make me thin and a whole new person.* As time passes and the disease of compulsive eating takes over, we feel the pain of failure. We may internalize the failure and blame ourselves for not having what it takes to succeed. While we might place the responsibility for success on the diet, interestingly enough, when the diet fails we often blame ourselves.

As compulsive eaters, we often look outside of ourselves for control. We may believe we have the ability to manage eating. We often vacillate between an ideal image of ourselves (perfectly in control) to the opposite image (totally out of control). As with alcoholism, denial prevents us from taking responsibility for the disease. Dieting is a symptom of the denial. The diet culture is a powerful foe to contend with. It is a big business; Americans spend about twenty billion dollars annually, looking for a solution to their weight problems. Quick weight loss schemes are a constant source of temptation. Our culture reinforces the belief that we can control our eating by taking a pill, buying the latest diet book, or buying special dietary foods.

The shift of responsibility from diets to ourselves is essential to the recovery process. While we did not ask for our disease, once it is diagnosed it is up to us to take the steps toward recovery. While there is no magical solution, there are resources to help us toward recovery.

What Is Recovery?

In order to begin a recovery program, we must first recognize that we suffer from a chronic, addictive disease. Attending Overeaters Anonymous, a Twelve Step group based on the principles of Alcoholics Anonymous, can help us recognize our disease and give us tools and support to aid us in our recovery. Professional therapy may add extra support. (It's important to seek a therapist who has an understanding of compulsive eating as a disease.)

A clear concept of abstinence, since it is the most difficult aspect of recovery, can help us progress. Abstinence is made easier if a realistic food and exercise program is planned. This book is intended to be of assistance in sound planning.

A recovery program means doing things one day at a time to help us live with our disease and to help us continue to discover ourselves as worthwhile people. This can involve any number of things:

- keeping a daily journal of happenings, of feelings or dreams;
- reading books that deal with self-growth, such as assertiveness and self-esteem;
- developing a relationship with a Higher Power (which reminds us that we are not in control of certain things in life);
- making daily meditation part of our lives;
- attending Twelve Step groups on a regular basis (which helps us reach out to people who share the same disease); and
- learning relapse symptoms.

Although recovery is work, it is challenging, rewarding, and offers you an opportunity to be free from the compulsion of food one day at a time.

nence Model for Compulsive Eaters

: alcoholics, who must learn to live *without* their drug of choice,
learn to live *with* ours.

The more we restrict specific foods from our diet the more likely we'll crave those foods and eventually give in to those cravings. Several studies have found a high correlation between restraint and binge eating; thus, food restriction may be an important prelude to binging.

This is a critical issue to explore. Food was the major focus in our lives before recovery; for at least a year into recovery, food must continue to be a major focus. But as we're in recovery, the focus shifts to positive management of eating. Once we feel confident about our new relationship with food, we can begin to concentrate on the other areas of recovery, including relationships with others, self-esteem, and spirituality. It is through abstinence that we gain a sense of strength in managing our relationship with food.

Let's examine a proposed abstinence model in each realm of the disease.

Physical Abstinence
- develop a sound food and exercise plan;
- pre-plan meals;
- do not count calories;
- stay off the bathroom scale;
- limit binge foods;
- limit high fat foods, refined sugars, and carbohydrates;
- abstain from dieting of any kind;
- abstain from eating between meals; and
- abstain from a sedentary lifestyle.

Emotional Abstinence
- abstain from negative self-talk and self-deprecating thoughts;
- abstain from pleasing others at the expense of your needs and feelings;
- abstain from shutting off feelings or minimizing feelings;
- abstain from isolating from others; and
- abstain from relationships that diminish your self-worth.

Spiritual Abstinence
- live life according to a personal value system;
- abstain from the belief that all things in life must be dealt with alone;
- develop a relationship with a Higher Power; and
- let go of control and realize that being in control does not guarantee a life of safety and freedom from pain.

Food Plans and Exercise Plans: How They Fit In

One area of abstinence we discussed relates to food and exercise plans. That is the major focus of this book. With an established food plan, we can feel more comfortable and confident in developing a recovery program in other areas.

Using alcoholism again as an example, alcoholics must first learn to live an alcohol-free life before they can begin to work on improving self-image, relationships, and spirituality. Similarly, we must have some success in managing our eating before dealing with spiritual and emotional recovery.

Most critical to developing a sound food and exercise plan are the words *flexible commitment.* This means we will give it our very best one day at a time.

Food and exercise plans are not static. They can change as our lifestyle changes. We can alter or modify a basic food and exercise plan for occasions, such as vacation times, restaurant eating, and celebrations.

Food and exercise plans can

- provide structure to daily eating needs;
- reduce anxiety about what and when to eat;
- help you identify your eating patterns in response to your feelings and experiences;
- help build confidence in taking responsibility for your life; and
- eliminate the need for diets.

Food and exercise plans are not

- diets;
- rigid; or
- intended to deprive.

While exercise is an important element in our recovery, it does not have to be drudgery or as challenging as a Jane Fonda workout. In the earlier stages of our recovery, it's helpful to share our food and exercise plans with a trusted food sponsor or a friend in our O.A. group. It's equally helpful to discuss how well we did on our previous day's plan. This sharing provides support and examination of difficult times and eating situations.

Chapter 1

Recovery Is a Process

Before developing a personal food and exercise recovery plan, it is recommended that you identify your current relationship with food, eating behaviors, and exercise habits by completing the Compulsive Eater's Behavior Inventory on pages 8-14. Place an "X" in the blank beside the statement that most accurately describes your response. **Note:** "x/week" means "times per week." For example: 2 to 3 x/week would read 2 to 3 times per week. Please do not total your score until you have completely finished the behavior inventory.

THE COMPULSIVE EATER'S BEHAVIOR INVENTORY

I. MEAL TIMING/FREQUENCY

1. I eat my first meal before noon.

_____	Never or rarely	0
_____	2 to 3 x/week	1
_____	4 to 6 x/week	2
_____	Every day	3

2. I eat after 7:00 P.M.

_____	Never or rarely	3
_____	2 to 3 x/week	2
_____	4 to 6 x/week	1
_____	Every day	0

3 I eat less than three times a day.

_____	Never or rarely	3
_____	2 to 3 x/week	2
_____	4 to 6 x/week	1
_____	Every day	0

4 I eat more than five times a day.

_____	Never or rarely	3
_____	2 to 3 x/week	2
_____	4 to 6 x/week	1
_____	Every day	0

Total _____

II. BINGE FOODS

1 I eat foods high in sugar: pop, cakes, sweetened cereals.

_____	Never or rarely	0
_____	4 or more x/day	1
_____	2 to 3 x/day	2
_____	1 x/day	3
_____	3 to 6 x/week	4

2. I eat foods high in fat: lunch meat, salad dressing, hot dogs, fried foods.

_____	Never or rarely	0
_____	4 or more x/day	1
_____	2 to 3 x/day	2
_____	1 x/day	3
_____	3 to 6 x/week	4

3. I eat at fast-food restaurants.

_____	Never or rarely	0
_____	4 or more x/day	1
_____	2 to 3 x/day	2
_____	1 x/day	3
_____	3 to 6 x/week	4

4. I eat snack foods: chips, pretzels, candy, and ice cream.

_____	Never or rarely	0
_____	4 or more x/day	1
_____	2 to 3 x/day	2
_____	1 x/day	3
_____	3 to 6 x/week	4

Total _____

III. BINGING

1. I pre-plan what foods I will eat.

_____	Never or rarely	0
_____	2 to 3 x/week	1
_____	4 to 6 x/week	2
_____	Every day	3

2. I count the calories in the foods I eat.

_____	Never or rarely	3
_____	2 to 3 x/week	2
_____	4 to 6 x/week	1
_____	Every day	0

3. I weigh myself.

_____	Never or rarely	3
_____	2 to 3 x/week	2
_____	4 to 6 x/week	1
_____	Every day	0

4. I follow a diet to help me lose weight.

_____	Never	3
_____	2 to 3 x/week	2
_____	4 to 6 x/week	1
_____	Every day	0

Total _____

THE COMPULSIVE EATER'S BEHAVIOR INVENTORY (Continued)

IV. ENVIRONMENT/FEELINGS

A. PLACE

1. I eat or drink in the car.

_____	Never or rarely	3
_____	2 to 4 x/week	2
_____	1 x/day	1
_____	2 or more x/day	0

2. I eat or drink while standing at the refrigerator.

_____	Never or rarely	3
_____	2.to 4 x/week	2
_____	1 x/day	1
_____	2 or more x/day	0

3. I eat while watching TV

_____	Never or rarely	3
_____	2 to 4 x/week	2
_____	1 x/day	1
_____	2 or more x/day	0

4. I limit my eating to only one room in the house. For example, the kitchen.

_____	Never or rarely	0
_____	2 to 4 x/week	1
_____	1 x/day	2
_____	2 or more x/day	3

Total _____

THE COMPULSIVE EATER'S BEHAVIOR INVENTORY (Continued)

B. HUNGER LEVEL

1. I eat when I feel physically hungry.

_____	Never or rarely	0
_____	2 to 4 x/week	1
_____	1 x/day	2
_____	2 or more x/day	3

2. I eat even when I am not very hungry.

_____	Never or rarely	3
_____	2 to 4 x/week	2
_____	1 x/day	1
_____	2 or more x/day	0

3. I eat because it is time to eat (for example, it's noon and that means lunch).

_____	Never or rarely	3
_____	2 to 4 x/week	2
_____	1 x/day	1
_____	2 or more x/day	0

4. I skip breakfast because I'm not hungry in the morning.

_____	Never or rarely	3
_____	2 to 3 x/week	2
_____	4 to 6 x/week	1
_____	Every day	0

5. I know when I'm physically hungry.

_____	Never or rarely	0
_____	2 to 4 x/week	1
_____	1 x/day	2
_____	2 or more x/day	3

Total _____

THE COMPULSIVE EATER'S BEHAVIOR INVENTORY (Continued)

C. MOOD

1. I eat when I am anxious or nervous.

	Never or rarely	3
_____	2 to 3 x/week	2
_____	4 to 6 x/week	1
_____	Every day	0

2. I eat when I am bored.

	Never or rarely	3
_____	2 to 3 x/week	2
_____	4 to 6 x/week	1
_____	Every day	0

3. I eat to relax.

	Never or rarely	3
_____	2 to 3 x/week	2
_____	4 to 6 x/week	1
_____	Every day	0

4. I eat in response to moods.

	Never or rarely	3
_____	2 to 3 x/week	2
_____	4 to 6 x/week	1
_____	Every day	0

Total _____

THE COMPULSIVE EATER'S BEHAVIOR INVENTORY (Continued)

V. PORTION SIZES

1. I eat serving sizes of meat, fish, or chicken at one meal that are four or more ounces.

   _____ Never or rarely   3
   _____ 2 to 4 x/week   2
   _____ 1 x/day   1
   _____ 2 or more x/day   0

2. I eat serving sizes of meat, fish, or chicken at one meal that are two to three ounces.

   _____ Never or rarely   0
   _____ 2 to 4 x/week   1
   _____ 1 x/day   2
   _____ 2 or more x/day   3

3. I eat serving sizes of starch (spaghetti, noodles, rice) at one meal in ½ cup quantities or greater.

   _____ Never or rarely   0
   _____ 2 to 4 x/week   1
   _____ 1 x/day   2
   _____ 2 or more x/day   3

4. I consume serving sizes of milk or yogurt at one meal that are in 1 cup (8 oz.) quantities.

   _____ Never or rarely   0
   _____ 2 to 4 x/week   1
   _____ 1 x/day   2
   _____ 2 or more x/day   3

5. I eat serving sizes of vegetables at one meal in ½ cup quantities or greater.

   _____ Never or rarely   0
   _____ 2 to 3 x/week   1
   _____ 1 x/day   2
   _____ 2 or more x/day   3

Total _____

THE COMPULSIVE EATER'S BEHAVIOR INVENTORY (Continued)

VI. EXERCISE/ACTIVITY

1. I do some type of exercise (for example, walking, biking, swimming) for 20 to 30 consecutive minutes.

_____	Never or rarely	0
_____	2 to 3 x/week	1
_____	4 to 6 x/week	2
_____	Every day	3

2. I monitor my heart rate when I exercise.

_____	Never or rarely	0
_____	2 to 3 x/week	1
_____	4 to 6 x/week	2
_____	Every day	3

3. I do some type of exercise such as gardening, painting, housework, chasing after kids.

_____	Never or rarely	0
_____	2 to 3 x/week	1
_____	4 to 6 x/week	2
_____	Every day	3

4. I make a special effort to include exercise in my daily routine (for example, using stairs instead of elevators, or parking the car far from store entrances).

_____	Never or rarely	0
_____	2 to 3 x/week	1
_____	4 to 6 x/week	2
_____	Every day	3

5. I exercise for 45 minutes or longer daily, 5 or more times per week, and feel guilty if I am unable to fit one of these exercise sessions into my schedule.

_____	Never or rarely	3
_____	2 to 3 x/week	2
_____	4 to 6 x/week	1
_____	Every day	0

Total _____

Scoring the Behavior Inventory

Go back to each category and circle the number 0, 1, 2, 3, or 4 next to each answer you've checked. For each group of questions, add up your scores and enter the score on the *Total* line.

Lower scores indicate behaviors linked to compulsive eating; higher scores represent behaviors associated with recovery from compulsive eating. Your scores for each category may be as low as 0, or as high as 16.

After you've scored your behavior inventory, review the categories in which you have low scores and high scores. Your scores may help you identify your relationships with food as well as eating and exercise behaviors that need changing. Keep in mind that abstinence commitments are long-range goals that are not expected to be met immediately. In this workbook, you'll be gradually developing a food and exercise plan.

The Abstinence in Action Recovery Plan

We believe that in order to change your relationship with food, your eating behaviors, and your exercise habits, your abstinence recovery plan must address and include the following:

Meals

Limit your food intake to no less but not more than three to four times per day. Eating only one or two times per day is counterproductive because this pattern encourages your body to make and store fat, increasing your number of fat cells. This is your body's way of storing energy to make it through the long time span between meals which it views as starvation. Your body also responds to these "starvation" periods between meals by slowing its metabolic rate so it can function on less energy from the food you eat and from the fat you've stored.

Eat more food early in the day: Get in your first meal before noon, and preferably before 9:30 A.M.

Set an evening cut-off time: 7:00 P.M. is a good point to stop eating for the day.

Binge Foods

Limit yourself to a total of two to three standard portions of sweets and high-fat foods per day, not two to three portions of each. For example, if you have a sweet roll at breakfast plus a hamburger and french fries from a fast-food restaurant at lunch, you have met your quota of sweets and foods high in fat for the day. This means that you would need to keep supper lean and avoid sweets the rest of the day.

We believe that by making certain foods *forbidden,* compulsive eaters increase their chances of binge eating. Part of recovery for the compulsive eater is learning to make *choices,* which involves having an open relationship with food instead of a closed one that defines certain foods as "good" or "bad."

"Good" foods are foods often seen by the compulsive eater as nonfattening and unlikely to promote a binge. Vegetables are usually considered "good" foods. Fruit, milk, cheese, yogurt, lean meats, and other protein foods may be considered "good" or "bad," depending on personal experience with these foods. More often, compulsive eaters identify sweets, bread and pasta, and foods high in fat as "bad" foods because they're seen as fattening and dangerous, possibly encouraging a binge.

Segregating foods into "good" and "bad" categories is an obstacle to the compulsive eater's recovery. Remember, recovery means changing your relationship with food and learning to make choices — not simply eliminating foods from your food plan.

Binging

Abstain from counting calories, weighing yourself on a frequent basis, and dieting. Pre-plan your food intake, allowing for flexibility of food choice.

Often, calorie counting, weighing oneself frequently (more than once a week), and dieting promote preoccupation with food and weight. When the compulsive eater exceeds a self-imposed calorie limit, gains any weight, or "cheats" by straying from a diet, the common reaction is, "I've blown it." "Blowing it" generally encourages binging and leads the compulsive eater into an uncomfortable relationship with food.

A healthy relationship with food is developed by planning food intake and allowing for flexibility of choices.

Environment and Feelings

Limit your eating and drinking to one room in your home and only do so while sitting rather than standing. Also, avoid combining other activities (watching television, driving, or reading) with eating or drinking. This will help you refrain from unconscious and secretive eating.

Focus on eating when you're physically hungry, and if you're in a bad mood, manage your urge to binge by limiting yourself to 50 to 75 percent of the quantity of food you ordinarily would eat. For example, if you're anxious or nervous and find yourself wanting to eat, get 50 to 75 percent of the food you usually would eat during a binge. Put the food on a plate or tray, sit down at a table, and while eating ask yourself, "Why am I eating this food and is it really making me feel any better?"

Asking yourself this question may prevent you from continuing to compulsively eat. In answering the question, you may begin to realize what moods trigger your compulsive eating episodes. An important part of your recovery is being aware of the moods that precipitate your compulsive eating so you can learn to manage your eating behavior.

Portion Sizes

Eat at least the minimum recommended number of portions per day from each of the following food categories:

- protein;
- dairy;
- fruits and vegetables;
- breads, grains, and starch; and
- fats.

Each food category fuels a major body function that will not perform as effectively if that particular body function relies on other foods. Consequently, it's essential that all food categories be included in your abstinence recovery plan.

Table I (page 18) lists the quantities of food recommended to help your body perform specific functions. While you're not limited to the listed minimum portions per day, you are urged to pre-plan your day's food intake to include the minimum number of portions before allowing for extra food from any one category. This helps assure that all body functions will be performed efficiently. Following these suggestions can be an effective tool in helping you learn to manage compulsive eating.

In Table I, the "One Portion" and the "Recommended Food Plan Distribution" information, especially for the protein and fats categories, should be viewed as guidelines and not hard, fast rules. For example, if you find it difficult to eat only two to three ounce portions of meat at a meal and

TABLE I
FOOD STRATEGY GUIDELINE

FOOD CATEGORY	FOODS INCLUDED	MAJOR BODY FUNCTION	ONE PORTION	MINIMUM RECOMMENDED PORTIONS PER DAY	RECOMMENDED FOOD PLAN DISTRIBUTION
PROTEIN	Meat, fish, chicken, turkey, eggs, cheese, cottage cheese, dried beans (cooked)	Builds and repairs body tissue	2 to 3 ounces	2 to 3	**Breakfast:** 1 to 2 ounces (optional) **Lunch and Supper:** 2 to 3 ounces at each meal
DAIRY	Milk, yogurt, cheese (*excluding cottage cheese and cream cheese*)	Keeps bones strong and healthy	8 ounces milk *or* 8 ounces yogurt *or* 1½ ounces cheese	2 to 3	**Breakfast:** One portion **Lunch and Supper:** One portion at one or both of these meals
FRUITS/ VEGETABLES	All fruits and vegetables: potatoes, tomatoes, carrots, broccoli, bananas, oranges, etc.	Keeps skin and eyes healthy. Helps the body resist and fight infection	Fruit: one medium piece *or* ½ cup fruit or juice Vegetables: ½ cup cooked *or* 1 cup raw	4	**Breakfast:** One portion fruit **Lunch** *Option I:* One portion fruit *Option II:* One portion fruit and vegetable **Supper** *Option I:* Two portions vegetable *Option II:* One portion vegetable
BREADS/ GRAINS/ STARCH	Bread, cereal, rice, macaroni, spaghetti, noodles, etc.	Supplies the body, especially the brain, with energy	1 slice bread *or* 1 ounce cold cereal *or* ½ cup cooked cereal, rice, spaghetti, noodles, etc. *or* ½ bagel *or* ½ English muffin	4 to 6	**Breakfast:** Two portions **Lunch and Supper:** One to two portions at both of these meals
OTHER/FATS	Margarine, salad dressing, and oil made from safflower, sunflower, corn, soybean, or cottonseed oil	Provides essential fatty acids for growth and skin. Helps vitamins A, D, E, and K to be absorbed	1 tsp. margarine or oil 1 tbsp. salad dressing 2 tsp. mayonnaise-type salad dressing	3	**Breakfast:** One portion **Lunch:** One portion **Supper:** One portion

you're used to five to ten ounces, focus on eating 50 to 75 percent of your usual protein portion. Exercising this option will help your food plan feel more personalized, comfortable, and realistic.

Remember, your goal is not to work toward eating only the minimum recommended portions per day from each food category. Instead, you should be striving for quantities of food from each category somewhere between your usual consumption and the minimum recommended level. This may help you to manage compulsive eating because you're taking responsibility for your food choices and this promotes an open relationship with food, and you're refraining from making yourself feel deprived.

If you limit your daily food intake to only the minimum number of portions in each category and you tend to eat the same foods rather than a variety, we recommend that you take a multivitamin/mineral supplement daily. Such a supplement should supply no more than 100 percent of the U.S. Recommended Daily Allowance for any of the vitamins and minerals listed.

Exercise and Activity

Include some type of exercise or activity in your schedule three to four days per week for 20 to 30 consecutive minutes each time.

It's important that you not begin exercising strenuously, especially if you're not used to exercising. If you haven't exercised in awhile or you have a special medical condition, such as high blood pressure, heart trouble, or diabetes, consult with your family doctor on your capacity to exercise.

Chapter 2

Food and Activity Records

We recommend that you record your food intake and activities daily. In doing this, we hope that you'll be more aware of your relationship with food, eating behaviors, and exercise habits. On page 22, Table II shows a Food and Activity Record you can use to record the information.

Here's an explanation of the type of information to record on your Food and Activity Record.

Date: At the beginning of each day, mark the appropriate date in the date box.

Time: Give the time of day you are eating.

Food: Name the food or drink.

Amount: Estimate either the weight of the food, the size of the portion, or the number of pieces (such as 1 tablespoon, 12 ounces, ¼ cup, 3 thin slices).

Place: Name of the room if at home, or if away, the restaurant, fast-food chain, or cafeteria.

Hunger: Record how hungry you felt just before eating. "0" means not hungry at all, and "5" means very hungry.

Mood: Describe your mood just before eating. Examples are happy, upset, neutral, bored, depressed, angry, tired, lonely, rushed.

Exercise: It is also a critical part of your physical abstinence recovery plan. It's a good idea to record the length of time (consecutive minutes) you exercise each day on your Food and Activity Record.

On page 23 is Table III — sample Food and Activity Record — which is an example of how to to complete the food segment of your records.

TABLE II
FOOD AND ACTIVITY RECORD

NAME: _____   _____ I EXERCISED FOR _____ CONSECUTIVE MINUTES

_____ I DID NOT EXERCISE

DATE	TIME	FOOD	AMOUNT	PLACE	HUNGER (0-5)	MOOD

TABLE III
SAMPLE FOOD AND ACTIVITY RECORD

NAME: _Jill Smith_ _____ ✓ I EXERCISED FOR ___15___ CONSECUTIVE MINUTES

_____ I DID NOT EXERCISE

DATE	TIME	FOOD	AMOUNT	PLACE	HUNGER (0-5)	MOOD
11/28	9:00a.m.	Coffee	1 cup			
		sugar	1 tsp.			
		powdered creamer	2 tsp.			
		Glazed Donuts	2 large			
	11:00 a.m.	Regular Cola	12 oz. can			
	12:30 p.m.	Hamburger on Bun	2 oz. meat 1 bun			
		French Fries	large order			
		Chocolate Shake	16 oz.			
	3:00 p.m.	Snickers Candy Bar	3.7 oz. bar			
	5:30 p.m.	Apple	1 medium			
	6:00 p.m.	Baked Chicken with Skin	4 oz. breast			
		Lettuce Salad with	2 cups lettuce			
		tomato	1 wedge			
		Reduced Calorie Blue	4 tbsp.			
		Cheese Salad Dressing				
		Mashed potatoes	½ cup			
		with gravy	2 tbsp.			
		Hot tea with	1 cup			
		sugar	1 tsp.			
	11:00 p.m.	Apple Pie with	¼ pie			
		vanilla ice cream	1 small scoop			

Commitment Contracts

Like the Food and Activity Record, the Commitment Contract (see Table IV on page 25) is an important part of this program. We recommend that you complete a Commitment Contract each week after you finish reading each chapter. Here's an explanation of how to fill out each line on the Commitment Contract:

Period of contract: Fill in the dates for one week. All contracts are to be made for one week periods only.

Goal: The goal is always twofold: (1) focusing on a food relationship or eating behavior, and (2) emphasizing an exercise activity. Choose an exercise activity you'll enjoy (perhaps you may wish to do two or three varied activities in a week's time to keep the exercise enjoyable). Set realistic goals. Contracts designed for two to four days are much more likely to be achieved than those set for five or more days. If after one or two weeks you haven't met your goals, set new ones or revise them.

Reward: The reward recognizes your achievements and makes the goals worthwhile. Rewards may be anything *except* food. They might be a bubble bath, movie, calling a friend long distance, or 30 minutes of quiet time to do whatever you want without feeling guilty. If you can't come up with an idea for a reward, you can always verbally congratulate yourself on your accomplishments.

Yes / No: After a one week contract has expired, put a check mark next to the "Yes" or "No" at the bottom of the contract, indicating whether you were able to meet your goal. A "no" may require that you reflect why the contract was not fulfilled so you can adjust the next week's contract.

TABLE IV
COMMITMENT CONTRACT

Name: _____

Period of Contract: From _____ to _____

1. **What is my goal?**

My goal is: _____

_____

_____

_____

_____

2. **What is my reward?**

If I achieve my goal, I may: _____

_____

_____

3. **If I do not achieve my goal, I agree that I will not receive my reward.**

Signed: _____

Date: _____

4. **I achieved my goal for this contract.**

_____ Yes

_____ No, explain: _____

_____

_____

TABLE V
SAMPLE COMMITMENT CONTRACT

Name: _Jill Smith_

Period of Contract: From _Nov. 11_ to _Nov. 18_

1. What is my goal?

My goal is: _(1) Two to three days out of the next week I will limit myself to eating 3 to 4 times per day. (2) I will walk for 10 to 15 consecutive minutes two to three days out of the next week._

2. What is my reward?

If I achieve my goal, I may: _Take 30 minutes to read a magazine without feeling guilty._

3. If I do not achieve my goal, I agree that I will not receive my reward.

Signed: _Jill Smith_

Date: _November 11_

4. I achieved my goal for this contract.

_____ Yes

_____ No, explain: _____

_____

_____

Low scores on the Compulsive Eater's Behavior Inventory can help you identify what food relationships and food behaviors you need to change, and what exercise habits you need to develop. In the Sample Commitment Contract (Table V), Jill reviewed the results of her behavior inventory and determined her low score of 5 on the Meal Timing and Frequency section indicated compulsive eating behavior. Other sections in which she received low scores included Binge Foods and Environment and Feelings. Consequently, Jill decided she needed to work aspects of these categories into her personal abstinence recovery plan.

To determine how she was going to change her relationship with food and her eating behaviors, Jill read the physical abstinence commitments in the Abstinence in Action Recovery Plan on page 15-17. After this review, Jill decided to focus on meal timing and frequency on her Commitment Contract. (See Table V to learn what food-related goal Jill selected.)

Jill then reviewed the Abstinence in Action Recovery Plan and the Exercise and Activity sections of her Compulsive Eater's Behavior Inventory for direction. Since she had no medical problems and enjoyed walking, she decided to walk for exercise (refer to Table V to see how Jill stated this goal on her Commitment Contract).

Jill needed to decide on a reward. She was used to rewarding herself with food, but decided that time to do something relaxing without feeling guilty would make her goals worth achieving (see Table V for the reward Jill chose).

Finally, Jill signed and dated her contract. At the end of her contract period (in a week's time) she will check "Yes" or "No," depending on whether she fulfilled the contract goals.

Using Table IV, take time now to complete a Commitment Contract for yourself for the upcoming week.

Chapter 3

Physical Measurements

Recording your physical measurements can help you assess your progress when you have completed the program described in this workbook. We ask that you weigh and measure yourself only twice during this program: now and at the end. Limiting these activities will help you abstain from repeated weight and measurement assessment, which can be compulsive behavior.

Take five to ten minutes to record your weight and physical measurements in the appropriate spaces in Table VI on page 30. Since it's difficult to measure yourself with a tape measure, ask a friend or family member with whom you feel comfortable to take and record these measurements. While there is no need to remove clothing, it would be helpful if you wear loose-fitting clothing.

Have all measurements taken on the right side of your body (this is primarily for the purpose of consistency). The following information will help the person who takes your measurements.

Upper Arm: Measure the arm at the halfway point between where the shoulder and arm connect, and the elbow.

Forearm: Measure the largest (thickest) region of the forearm.

Wrist: Measure the arm just slightly to the upper side of the bony projection on the wrist.

Chest: Measure around the chest through the middle of the nipples.

Waist: It is easiest for you to indicate where your waist area is. If you're uncertain where your waist is, bend your upper body to the side and measure the creased region.

Hips: Stand with your feet as close together as is comfortably possible. Measure the fullest area of the hip region.

Thigh: Measure the largest (thickest) area of the upper leg region.

TABLE VI
BODY PART MEASUREMENTS

I. INITIAL MEASUREMENTS

Starting Date:_____

Weight: _____

Body Part Circumference Measures (Right side of body)

Upper Arm _____   Waist _____

Forearm _____   Hip _____

Wrist _____   Thigh _____

Chest _____

II. FINAL MEASUREMENTS

Completion Date:_____

Weight: _____

Body Part Circumference Measures (Right side of body)

Upper Arm _____   Waist _____

Forearm _____   Hip _____

Wrist _____   Thigh _____

Chest _____

Assignment

1. Before beginning Chapter Four, fill out the Food and Activity Records (on the following pages) for the next seven days.

2. During the upcoming week, focus on achieving the food and exercise goals you identified for yourself on your Commitment Contract (see Table IV).

3. Wait seven days before reading Chapter Four.

FOOD AND ACTIVITY RECORD

NAME: _____   _____ I EXERCISED FOR _____ CONSECUTIVE MINUTES

_____ I DID NOT EXERCISE

DATE	TIME	FOOD	AMOUNT	PLACE	HUNGER (0-5)	MOOD

ABSTINENCE IN ACTION

FOOD AND ACTIVITY RECORD

NAME: _____   _____ I EXERCISED FOR _____ CONSECUTIVE MINUTES

_____ I DID NOT EXERCISE

DATE	TIME	FOOD	AMOUNT	PLACE	HUNGER (0-5)	MOOD

FOOD AND ACTIVITY RECORD

NAME: _____   _____ I EXERCISED FOR _____ CONSECUTIVE MINUTES

_____ I DID NOT EXERCISE

DATE	TIME	FOOD	AMOUNT	PLACE	HUNGER (0-5)	MOOD

ABSTINENCE IN ACTION

FOOD AND ACTIVITY RECORD

NAME: _____   _____ I EXERCISED FOR _____ CONSECUTIVE MINUTES

_____ I DID NOT EXERCISE

DATE	TIME	FOOD	AMOUNT	PLACE	HUNGER (0-5)	MOOD

FOOD AND ACTIVITY RECORD

NAME: _____   _____ I EXERCISED FOR _____ CONSECUTIVE MINUTES

_____ I DID NOT EXERCISE

DATE	TIME	FOOD	AMOUNT	PLACE	HUNGER (0-5)	MOOD

ABSTINENCE IN ACTION

FOOD AND ACTIVITY RECORD

NAME: _____   _____ I EXERCISED FOR _____ CONSECUTIVE MINUTES

_____ I DID NOT EXERCISE

DATE	TIME	FOOD	AMOUNT	PLACE	HUNGER (0-5)	MOOD

FOOD AND ACTIVITY RECORD

NAME: _____   _____ I EXERCISED FOR _____ CONSECUTIVE MINUTES

_____ I DID NOT EXERCISE

DATE	TIME	FOOD	AMOUNT	PLACE	HUNGER (0-5)	MOOD

ABSTINENCE IN ACTION

Chapter 4

Food and Exercise Facts

First, let's briefly review the material covered in the previous chapters. You were introduced to several possibilities for changing your relationship with food, your eating behaviors, and your exercise habits as part of your physical abstinence recovery plan. In addition, you also kept your first set of food records and explored the time of day you eat, the types and amounts of food you eat, where you eat, how physically hungry you are when you eat, what mood you are in when you eat, and the amount of exercise you do.

Keeping the food records may help you evaluate whether you met the goals you set for yourself on your first Commitment Contract. (We'll take a more in-depth look at your Commitment Contract goals at the end of this chapter.)

Exercise

There are many reasons why exercise is helpful in weight management and a food planning program. Here are seven major benefits of exercise for permanent weight management:

1. Exercise burns calories immediately.
2. Exercise speeds up metabolism. Exercising for 20 to 30 minutes consecutively may help a person burn calories up to 25 percent faster than normal for 15 hours after the exercise is completed.
3. Exercise dulls your appetite for 30 to 60 minutes. For example, exercising shortly before a meal can help prevent a person from overeating.
4. Exercise prevents the body's metabolism from slowing down. Dieting alone to lose weight causes the body's metabolism to slow down.

5. Exercise prevents muscle loss. Of total weight lost, 35 to 40 percent may be muscle tissue when weight is lost by calorie restriction alone. Muscle tissue is the main calorie burner in the body; this is not tissue a person should lose.

6. Exercise promotes loss of fat tissue and an increase in the proportion of lean muscle tissue.

7. Exercise can relieve stress and tension. Exercise as a stress release can help you abstain from compulsive eating and prevent weight gain.

Body Composition

Let's examine the difference between fat weight and muscle weight. Here's a picture of Steve and Tom. Steve and Tom are the same age and height, but who do you think weighs more?

WHO WEIGHS MORE?

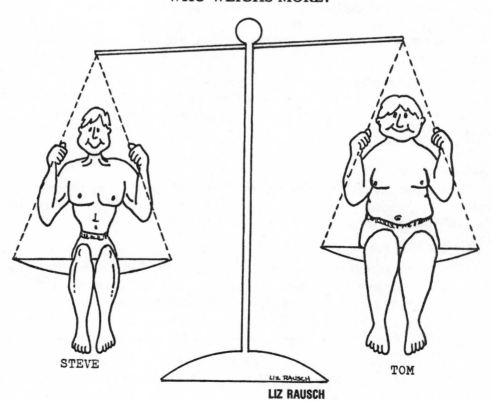

STEVE

TOM

LIZ RAUSCH

ABSTINENCE IN ACTION

Answer: Steve and Tom are not only the same age and height, but also the same weight. Nevertheless, their body compositions are different. Steve has significantly more lean muscle tissue than Tom, who has a higher percent of unhealthy fat tissue.

Muscle tissue weighs more than fat tissue, so it would seem logical that Steve would weigh more than Tom. But Tom has enough extra fat weight to compensate for the heaviness of Steve's lean muscle tissue, so Steve and Tom weigh the same.

If you are diligent about following both the food and exercise components of your physical abstinence recovery plan, you may experience limited weight loss, but a significant change in your physical measurements may be noticed. In other words, the scale may not say you have changed, but your clothes will fit much better.

Primarily due to exercise, you may replace flabby fat tissue with lean, firm, healthy muscle tissue. More than what the scale says, a change in your body measurements is a better indicator that your physical abstinence recovery plan is working.

Although Tom has a lot of fat weight and may look like he eats more than Steve, Steve actually eats more calories than Tom because muscle tissue burns greater amounts of calories than fat tissue.

Types of Exercise

There are two types of exercise: (1) those that will promote weight loss, and (2) those that improve muscle flexibility, strength, and tone.

Exercises that promote weight loss are known as aerobic exercises. These include exercises or activities (jogging, fast walking, biking, swimming, dancing, or using a rowing machine) that keep your heart beating at your working heart rate level (which is based on your age and level of fitness) for at least fifteen consecutive minutes.

Although exercises or activities that help give your muscles strength and make them more flexible and firm are valuable, they won't promote weight loss. This is because these exercises (weight lifting, slow walking, golf, sit-ups, softball, gardening, or housework) don't cause your heart to beat at your working heart rate level for fifteen consecutive minutes.

Monitoring Your Heart Rate During Exercise

It's important to monitor your heart rate while you're exercising to make sure you're getting the most out of the exercise without risking damage to your heart. You can monitor your heart rate during exercise by using the conversation check test, or by testing your working heart rate level. The "conversation check test" means that you should be able to talk comfortably while you're exercising; if you can't, then you need to exercise less vigorously until you reach this point.

Monitoring your working heart rate level is a more precise technique for ensuring that you're getting the maximum benefit out of exercise without overtaxing your heart muscle and possibly compromising your health.

The working heart rate (WHR) or the training pulse rate is the heart rate level you should reach in an aerobic workout to increase your level of fitness. The WHR is figured by multiplying the difference between 220 and your age by 60 percent (for two months); 70 percent (for another two months); and 80 percent (for another couple months); and 80 to 85 percent (thereafter).

Example: 220 Constant
− 32 Exerciser's age
188 Difference = maximum pulse rate
× .60 Percent maximum pulse rate
112.80 Rounded = 110, the working heart rate. The exerciser's pulse rate should be 110 beats per minute; about 18 beats in ten seconds.

Table VII identifies the WHR for individuals at various ages and levels of fitness. The figures in Table VII are based on the formula previously described.

TABLE VII
<u>WORKING HEART RATE</u>

AGE	WHR-1 Beats/min, Beats/10 sec	WHR-2 Beats/min, Beats/10 sec
Under 30	120 = 20	140 = 23
30-44	110 = 18	130 = 22
45-60	100 = 17	120 = 20
Over 60	100 = 17	110 = 18

AGE	WHR-3	WHR-4
Under 30	150 = 25	150-160 = 25-27
30-44	140 = 23	140-150 = 23-25
45-60	130 = 22	130-140 = 22-23
Over 60	120 = 20	120-130 = 20-22

WHR   = Working Heart Rate
WHR-1 = WHR for the first 8 weeks — about 60 percent maximum pulse rate
WHR-2 = WHR for the second 8 weeks — about 70 percent maximum pulse rate
WHR-3 = WHR for the third 8 weeks — about 80 percent maximum pulse rate
WHR-4 = WHR for 80-85 percent maximum rate to maintain total fitness

Taking Your Pulse

Using your index and middle fingers, you can find your pulse on the thumb side of your wrist or the side of your neck. Do not take your pulse with your thumb, because it has a pulse of its own and you may get a double count.

Count your pulse while watching the second hand of a watch for ten seconds and compare this number with the appropriate Beats/10 Seconds column in the Working Heart Rate table. It's important to monitor the intensity of the exercise so that you are meeting, but not exceeding, your WHR based on your age and level of fitness. This action will help guarantee that you're getting the maximum benefit out of exercise without risking damage to your heart.

During an aerobic exercise, you should stop to monitor your heart rate about three times: (1) two to three minutes into the activity, (2) midway through the activity, and (3) at or near the end of the exercise.

It's a good idea to compare your heart rate taken on the side of your neck with that taken on the thumb side of your wrist. If, on several occasions, your neck pulse count is *lower* than your wrist count, you should use the wrist count to monitor your working heart rate.

Caution: People who work their heart rate above their working rates can damage their hearts and possibly have heart attacks. Individuals at particular risk would include men over age 40, adults not used to following a regular exercise program, and those with heart-related health problems.

You should increase your working heart rate from one level to another only if you have been performing an aerobic activity, such as aerobic dancing, for a minimum of 20 to 30 consecutive minutes, three to four times per week for eight consecutive weeks.

Now that you have reviewed all the aspects of monitoring your heart rate during exercise, take a few minutes to determine your working heart rate and to count your pulse.

Remember, if you have a medical condition (especially back problems, heart disease, high blood pressure, or diabetes) or you are not used to exercising, check with your doctor regarding your capacity for exercise. Ask your physician if the working heart rate you have calculated for yourself is appropriate.

Commitment Contract Review

Notice in Table VIII (Sample Commitment Contract) that Jill checked the "yes" under item 4. This means that she was able to limit herself to eating three to four times daily for at least two days during the past week. In addition, she had checked her food and activity records on the three days that she had walked at least ten to fifteen minutes. As a result, Jill had met the goals of her Commitment Contract and could have her reward: 30 minutes to read a magazine.

Take five to ten minutes to review your food and exercise records to determine whether you achieved the goals on your Commitment Contract. If you met your goals, follow through with your reward. If you didn't meet the goals, ask yourself, *why?* Were the goals unrealistic? How could the goals have been designed to be more achievable?

Commitment Contract: Upcoming Week

Take a few minutes to use Table IX on page 48 to design a Commitment Contract for the next seven days. If you met your contract goals for the past week, you may want to keep them the same since this is only the second week and you know your goals were achievable. Since the emphasis of this chapter is exercise, it's recommended that you include monitoring your heart rate in this week's contract. For example: "I will walk for three days out of the next week and I will monitor my working heart rate level each time."

Focusing on too many goals at once can set you up for failure. Focusing on a limited number of goals and achieving them will build your self-confidence and help you develop a comfortable recovery plan.

If you feel confident about adding another food relationship or food behavior goal to your contract, then use your past week's food records and a comparison of your Compulsive Eater's Behavior Inventory against the Abstinence in Action Recovery Plan (described in Chapter One) to guide you in selecting a realistic goal.

If you didn't meet your goals the past week, use the same goals or a revised edition. You may choose different goals, especially if the past week's goals were overwhelming. Once again, your past week's food records and a comparison of your Compulsive Eater's Behavior Inventory against the Abstinence in Action Recovery Plan are two tools for designing goals. Be sure to incorporate monitoring your heart rate into your exercise goal.

Assignment

1. Fill out the Food and Activity Records on page 49-55 each day for the next seven days.

2. Focus on achieving the food and exercise goals you identified for yourself for the upcoming week on your Commitment Contract.

3. Wait seven days before reading Chapter Five.

TABLE VIII
SAMPLE COMMITMENT CONTRACT

Name: _Jill Smith_

Period of Contract: From _Nov. 11_ to _November 18_

1. What is my goal?

My goal is: _(1) Two to three days out of the next week I will limit myself to eating 3 to 4 times per day. (2) I will walk for 10 to 15 consecutive minutes 2 to 3 days out of the next week._

2. What is my reward?

If I achieve my goal, I may: _Take 30 minutes to read a magazine without feeling guilty._

3. If I do not achieve my goal, I agree that I will not receive my reward.

Signed: _Jill Smith_

Date: _November 11_

4. I achieved my goal for this contract.

____✔____ Yes

_____ No, explain: _____

_____

_____

TABLE IX
COMMITMENT CONTRACT

Name: _____

Period of Contract: From _____ to _____

1. What is my goal?

My goal is: _____

_____

_____

_____

_____

2. What is my reward?

If I achieve my goal, I may: _____

_____

_____

3. If I do not achieve my goal, I agree that I will not receive my reward.

Signed: _____

Date: _____

4. I achieved my goal for this contract.

_____ Yes

_____ No, explain: _____

_____

_____

FOOD AND ACTIVITY RECORD

NAME: _____   _____ I EXERCISED FOR _____ CONSECUTIVE MINUTES

_____ I DID NOT EXERCISE

DATE	TIME	FOOD	AMOUNT	PLACE	HUNGER (0-5)	MOOD

FOOD AND ACTIVITY RECORD

NAME: _____   _____ I EXERCISED FOR _____ CONSECUTIVE MINUTES

_____ I DID NOT EXERCISE

DATE	TIME	FOOD	AMOUNT	PLACE	HUNGER (0-5)	MOOD

ABSTINENCE IN ACTION

FOOD AND ACTIVITY RECORD

NAME: _____   _____ I EXERCISED FOR _____ CONSECUTIVE MINUTES

_____ I DID NOT EXERCISE

DATE	TIME	FOOD	AMOUNT	PLACE	HUNGER (0-5)	MOOD

FOOD AND ACTIVITY RECORD

NAME: _____   _____ I EXERCISED FOR _____ CONSECUTIVE MINUTES

_____ I DID NOT EXERCISE

DATE	TIME	FOOD	AMOUNT	PLACE	HUNGER (0-5)	MOOD

FOOD AND ACTIVITY RECORD

NAME: _____   _____ I EXERCISED FOR _____ CONSECUTIVE MINUTES

_____ I DID NOT EXERCISE

DATE	TIME	FOOD	AMOUNT	PLACE	HUNGER (0-5)	MOOD

FOOD AND ACTIVITY RECORD

NAME: _____   _____ I EXERCISED FOR _____ CONSECUTIVE MINUTES

_____ I DID NOT EXERCISE

DATE	TIME	FOOD	AMOUNT	PLACE	HUNGER (0-5)	MOOD

ABSTINENCE IN ACTION

FOOD AND ACTIVITY RECORD

NAME: _____   _____ I EXERCISED FOR _____ CONSECUTIVE MINUTES

_____ I DID NOT EXERCISE

DATE	TIME	FOOD	AMOUNT	PLACE	HUNGER (0-5)	MOOD

Chapter 5

Trim the Fat: Part I

The last chapter focused on exercise. You learned that there are many benefits of exercise related to permanent weight management, beyond burning calories. By exploring the relationship between exercise, body composition, and weight management, you learned the benefits of including exercise in your physical abstinence recovery plan.

This chapter will help you become more aware of the fat content in foods and why cutting high-fat foods from your menu is an important aspect of changing your eating behaviors.

Let's take a look at five major benefits of cutting back on the amount of fat you eat. They include:

- Reducing your calorie intake fairly quickly.
- Encouraging your body to lower its set point weight (a certain weight your body is accustomed to).
- Causing more calories to be burned in your body.
- Decreasing, maybe, your risk of developing certain types of cancer.
- Reducing your risk of developing heart disease.

Let's explore these benefits in greater detail.

Benefit One

Cutting back on fat reduces your calorie intake fairly quickly.

The calories in food are derived from three basic nutrients: carbohydrate, protein, and fat. Looking at a food label makes this clear. Look at the food label on the next page for Philadelphia Cream Cheese.

SAMPLE FOOD LABEL

PHILADELPHIA CREAM CHEESE
Nutrition Information Per serving

Serving Size .1 oz.
Serving Per Pkg 8
Calories. 100
Protein 2g
Carbohydrate 1g
Fat 10g

Percentage of U.S. Recommended
Daily Allowances: Protein
4, Vitamin A 6, Riboflavin 2,
Calcium 2; Contains less than 2
percent of U.S.RDA of Vitamin C,
Thiamine, Niacin, Iron.
Ingredients: Pasteurized milk and cream
cheese culture, salt, carob bean gum.

Notice that there are 2 grams of protein, 1 gram of carbohydrate, and 10 grams of fat in a one ounce serving of the cheese.

Now look at the "Label Interpretation." Follow the directions for translating grams into calories for protein, carbohydrates, and fat.

Label Interpretation

To understand the "gram" information on a food label, it is helpful to translate the grams into calories. First you need to know that both carbohydrates and protein have four calories per gram; fat has nine calories per gram. Right away this tells you that fat is the richest source of calories since it contains two and one half times more calories than either carbohydrates or protein.

This point is further illustrated by multiplying the grams of carbohydrate, protein, and fat on the sample food label by the calories per gram. Let's figure this out together:

- 2 grams protein × 4 calories per gram of protein = 8 calories in one serving of cream cheese from protein.
- 1 gram carbohydrate × 4 calories per gram of carbohydrate = 4 calories in one serving of cream cheese come from carbohydrate.
- 10 grams fat × 9 calories per gram of fat = 90 calories in one serving of cream cheese come from fat.

ABSTINENCE IN ACTION

Note: The food label says 100 calories per serving instead of 102 calories due to the rounding of numbers, which is allowed on food labels.

Since fat is a high source of calories, if we limit the quantity of foods we eat that are high in fat, we can cut calories without having to count them. Abstaining from calorie counting is recommended, since it is a binge behavior.

Benefit Two

Cutting back on fat encourages your body to lower its set point weight.

There is a theory that the set point weight is the weight the body feels most comfortable maintaining. In other words, the set point weight works similarly to your house thermostat.

For example, if you set your house thermostat at 72 degrees in the winter, the thermostat triggers the furnace to turn on if the temperature drops below 72 degrees. Once the temperature reaches 72 degrees, the thermostat triggers the furnace to shut off until the thermostat once again senses that the temperature is below 72 degrees.

Your set point weight, much like a thermostat, helps you maintain a certain weight to which your body is accustomed. If you either lose or gain over your set point weight, you'll either want to increase or decrease your eating and physical activity so that your weight returns to your body's set point weight.

Just as your home thermostat setting can be altered, so can your set point weight. For example, eating high-fat foods for a long period of time can lead to a higher set point weight. Continually eating foods low in fat can help your body to redefine its set point weight to a lower level. A regular program of exercise may also help you lower your set point weight.

Benefit Three

Cutting back on fat causes more calories to be burned in your body.

A calorie is a calorie, whether it comes from fat, protein, or carbohydrates, was the popular belief. Lately more and more evidence shows that fat calories are more difficult for the body to burn than carbohydrate calories. Apparently, the body prefers to burn carbohydrates for energy and store fat from food in the body's fat cells. Consequently, the body spends less energy (calories) to process fat than carbohydrates. It would appear that to eat high-fat foods causes fewer calories to be burned; eating low-fat, high-carbohydrate foods causes more calories to be used.

Benefits Four and Five

Cutting back on fat may decrease your risk of developing certain types of cancer and reduce your risk of developing heart disease.

Eating too much fat of any kind may increase chances of contracting cancer of the colon, breast, prostate, or endometrium (the mucous membrane lining the uterus). Therefore, reducing your intake of fat may decrease your risk of getting these types of cancer. Further, cutting back on fat can reduce your risk of heart attack.

Keep in mind that there are several factors involved in the development of cancer and heart attacks and a high-fat diet is only one of those factors. While avoiding a high-fat intake doesn't guarantee that you won't get cancer or have a heart attack, it is one factor that you can control, at least reducing your risk of disease. Many nutritionists and health organizations (such as the American Heart Association) recommend that you keep your day's total fat consumption to approximately 30 percent of total calories consumed.

Getting To Know Your Fat

There are many good reasons to cut your fat consumption. However, other than cream cheese, do you know what foods are high in fat? Look at the Getting to Know Your Fat Worksheet on page 61. Take a few minutes to rate each of the 25 foods on the worksheet as high, medium, or low in fat. For example, if you think a poached egg is high in fat, place a check in the "high" column.

After rating the food for fat content, ask yourself if you think the food is fattening, based on your personal definition of this term. For example, if you think an egg is fattening, then put a check in the "yes" column.

When you have completed the Getting to Know Your Fat Worksheet, compare your answers against the answer key that follows.

GETTING TO KNOW YOUR FAT WORKSHEET

Food Item	High	Medium	Low	Fattening? yes/no
1. A poached egg				
2. Whole wheat bread, one slice				
3. Chicken breast from Kentucky Fried Chicken, 1 piece				
4. Orange, 1 medium				
5. Bacon, cooked, 1 strip				
6. Peanut butter, 2 tbsp.				
7. Frozen corn, cooked, ½ cup				
8. Hamburger patty, 4 oz. broiled				
9. Sugar-free Cafe Vienna coffee by General Food International Coffees, 6 oz. serving				
10. Sesame seeds, 2 tbsp.				
11. Pepperoni pizza, 1 piece from medium pizza				
12. Tuna, water-packed, 3 oz.				
13. M&M's plain chocolate candy, 1 package				
14. Macaroni, ½ cup plain				
15. Whole milk, 8 oz.				
16. Turkey hot dogs, 1				
17. American cheese, 1 oz.				
18. Banana, 1 whole				
19. Corn oil margarine, 2 tsp.				
20. Salad dressing, 1 tbsp.				
21. Reduced-calorie salad dressing, less oil, 1 tbsp.				
22. Apple pie, ⅛ of 9-inch pie				
23. Croutons, ½ cup				
24. Coconut, 2 tbsp.				
25. Fish sticks, 2 sticks				

GETTING TO KNOW YOUR FAT WORKSHEET
(ANSWER KEY)

Food Item	High	Medium	Low	Fattening? yes/no
1. A poached egg	✔			✔
2. Whole wheat bread, one slice			✔	✔
3. Chicken breast from Kentucky Fried Chicken, 1 piece	✔			✔
4. Orange, 1 medium			✔	✔
5. Bacon, cooked, 1 strip	✔			✔
6. Peanut butter, 2 tbsp.	✔			✔
7. Frozen corn, cooked, ½ cup			✔	✔
8. Hamburger patty, 4 oz. broiled	✔			✔
9. Sugar-free Cafe Vienna coffee by General Food International Coffees, 6 oz. serving	✔			✔
10. Sesame seeds, 2 tbsp.	✔			✔
11. Pepperoni pizza, 1 piece from medium pizza	✔			✔
12. Tuna, water-packed, 3 oz.			✔	✔
13. M&M's plain chocolate candy, 1 package	✔			✔
14. Macaroni, ½ cup plain			✔	✔
15. Whole milk, 8 oz.	✔			✔
16. Turkey hot dogs, 1	✔			✔
17. American cheese, 1 oz.	✔			✔
18. Banana, 1 whole			✔	✔
19. Corn oil margarine, 2 tsp.	✔			✔
20. Salad dressing, 1 tbsp.	✔			✔
21. Reduced-calorie salad dressing, less oil, 1 tbsp.	✔			✔
22. Apple pie, ⅛ of 9-inch pie		✔		✔
23. Croutons, ½ cup	✔ with butter		✔ without butter	✔
24. Coconut, 2 tbsp.	✔			✔
25. Fish sticks, 2 sticks	✔			✔

Surprised? The answer to the "fattening" question is "no" for every food, in the quantity given, on the fat worksheet. It isn't fair to label foods as fattening, especially in small or normal sized portions. It's more important to consider the whole day's food intake than focusing on one food or one meal. Foods don't become fattening until eaten in quantities beyond your body's daily total calorie need. Keep in mind that two large carrots, about 80 calories, can be fattening if they are eaten at the end of the day when your body's need for calories has been satisfied.

Now you are familiar with the fat content of at least 25 foods, but what about all the other foods you eat?

Look at the Trimming Fat and Refined Sugar information below and on the next two pages. Notice that the foods and beverages have been placed in categories (Featherweights, Lightweights, Middleweights, Heavyweights, and Super Heavyweights) based on their total fat and refined sugar content. The foods and beverages in the Featherweight, Lightweight, and Middleweight categories are the best selections because they are lowest in fat or refined sugar content. It is best to limit (not omit) your intake of foods and beverages in the Heavyweight and Super Heavyweight categories, because they are high in total fat or refined sugar. You should limit your intake of foods high in refined sugar because they tend to be high in calories and low in food value.

TRIMMING FAT AND REFINED SUGAR
BEVERAGES

I. Featherweights

Diet pop
Water (spring, tap, Perrier)
Kool Aid with NutraSweet
Coffee
Tea

II. Lightweights

Skim milk
1 percent milk
Buttermilk made with 1 percent milk

III. Middleweights

2 percent milk
100 percent fruit juice

IV. Heavyweights

3.25 percent fat milk, also known as
    whole milk
Chocolate milk
General Foods International Coffees, both
    regular and sugar free
Milk shakes

V. Super Heavyweights

Regular pop
Regular Kool Aid
Fruit drinks
Beer
Wine and liquor

FOODS

I. Featherweights

Dill pickles
Mustard
Air-popped popcorn
Herbs and spices
Oil-free, low calorie salad dressing

II. Lightweights

1. *Vegetables:*
   Plain

2. *Fruit:*
   Fresh, except avocado
   Canned, in fruit juice or water

3. *Grains:*
   Noodles
   Rice
   Spaghetti
   Bread
   Macaroni
   Buns
   Unsweetened cereals, except granola

4. *Protein/Main Course:*
   Chicken, white meat (no skin)
   Turkey, white meat (no skin)
   Tofu
   1 percent milk fat cottage cheese
   Tuna packed in water
   Seafood: scallops and shrimp
   Fish: perch
   Dried peas, beans, and lentils
   Low-fat plain yogurt

5. *Soups:*
   Chicken noodle, vegetable, tomato
   (remove visible fat from can)

III. Middleweights

1. *Vegetables*: See Lightweights

2. *Fruit*: See Lightweights

3. *Grains:*
   Pancakes, prepared in a little oil
   Popcorn popped in a little oil but no
   added fat after cooking
   Biscuits, plain
   Wheat germ, plain
   Corn bread

4. *Protein/Main Course:*
   Chicken, dark meat
   Turkey, dark meat, ground turkey
   Some cheese products: Borden Lite-Line
   or Weight Watchers
   Delicatessen meats:
   Turkey breast, turkey ham, turkey
   pastrami
   Chicken breast
   Frozen dinners: many of the Lean
   Cuisine, Weight Watchers, Light and
   Elegant, et cetera (figure 30 percent
   fat or less)
   Veal: loin, round, or shoulder
   Beef: flank steak, ground round, lean
   chuck pot roast
   Fish: flounder, haddock, halibut
   Yogurt: vanilla, coffee, or lemon
   (1.5 percent milk fat or less)

FOODS (Cont.)

IV: Heavyweights

1. *Vegetables:* with cheese or cream sauces

2. *Fruit:* canned in heavy syrup, dried

3. *Grains:* sweetened cereals, granola

4. *Protein/Main Course:*
   Turkey bologna, salami
   Chicken, roasted with skin
   Turkey hot dogs
   Chicken hot dogs
   Tuna in oil
   Chili
   Eggs
   TV dinners and pot pies
   Fish: salmon, sardines, mackerel, and fried fish
   Cheese: blue, cheddar, American, Swiss, Monterey Jack, et cetera
   Ground chuck
   Lasagna
   Ham, lean
   Lamb chops
   Yogurt with fruit

5. *Soups:* cream soups

6. *Miscellaneous:*
   Ice cream
   Pudding
   Reduced calorie salad dressings

V. Super Heavyweights

1. *Vegetables:* See Lightweights and Heavyweights

2. *Fruit:* Processed fruit rolls and fruit roll snack foods, avocado

3. *Grains:* See Lightweights, Middleweights, and Heavyweights

4. *Protein/Main Course:*
   Bratwurst
   Hot dogs (beef and pork)
   Sausage
   Bacon
   Hamburger
   Peanut butter
   Luncheon meats (bologna, salami, et cetera)
   Fish sticks
   Meat pizza

5. *Soups:* See Heavyweights and Lightweights

6. *Miscellaneous:*
   Nuts
   Seeds: pumpkin, sesame, sunflower
   Chocolate

Cream cheese	Olives
Oil	Coconut
Sherbet	Cakes
Jelly	Pies
Honey	Cookies
Syrup	Pastry
Doughnuts	Cream
Sweet pickles	Gravy
Salad dressing	Butter
Popsicles	Margarine
Mayonnaise	Potato Chips
Candy	

Commitment Contract Review

Review your food and activity records from this past week to determine whether you achieved your Commitment Contract goals. Follow through with your reward if you met your goals. If you were unable to meet the goals, ask yourself "why?" Were the goals too unrealistic? How could the goals have been designed to be more achievable?

Commitment Contract: Upcoming Week

Take a few minutes to use Table X on page 67 to design a Commitment Contract for the next seven days. If you met your Commitment Contract goals for the past week, continue to include them on this week's contract.

As a result of our focus this week, try adding a food behavior goal regarding reducing fat from the foods you eat. Based on the information presented in the Abstinence in Action Recovery Plan regarding binge foods on pages 15-16, try limiting yourself to two to three portions of high-fat foods for two to three days out of the next seven. If you feel this is too unrealistic, you may want to focus on a particular high-fat food that you use often and reduce your consumption of it (for example, butter or margarine) by 25 to 50 percent for two to three days. Refer to Table XI on page 68 for a Sample Commitment Contract for a goal regarding fat intake.

If you didn't meet your goals for the past week, use the same goals, revise them, or focus on completely different goals. For example, you may only want to focus on foods high in fat and an activity goal.

TABLE X
COMMITMENT CONTRACT

Name: _____

Period of Contract: From _____ to _____

1. What is my goal?

My goal is: _____

_____

_____

_____

_____

2. What is my reward?

If I achieve my goal, I may: _____

_____

_____

3. If I do not achieve my goal, I agree that I will not receive my reward.

Signed: _____

Date: _____

4. I achieved my goal for this contract.

_____ Yes

_____ No, explain: _____

_____

_____

TABLE XI
SAMPLE COMMITMENT CONTRACT

Name: _Jill Smith_

Period of Contract: From _December 1_ to _December 8_

1. What is my goal?

My goal is: _(1) 2 to 3 days out of the next week I will limit myself to eating 3 to 4 times per day. (2) 2 to 3 days out of the next week I will limit myself to 2 to 3 high fat foods (Heavy & Super Heavy weights). (3) I will walk for 15 consecutive minutes 3 days out of the next week and I will monitor my heart rate to my working heart rate level each time._

2. What is my reward?

If I achieve my goal, I may: _go to see a movie._

_____

_____

3. If I do not achieve my goal, I agree that I will not receive my reward.

Signed: _Jill Smith_

Date: _December 1_

4. I achieved my goal for this contract.

_____ Yes

_____ No, explain: _____

_____

_____

Assignment

1. Fill out Food and Activity Records (on the following pages) each day for the next seven days.

2. Focus on meeting the food and exercise goals you chose for yourself for the upcoming week.

3. Wait seven days before reading Chapter Six.

4. Familiarize yourself with the foods and beverages that fall into each of the following categories: Featherweights, Lightweights, Middleweights, Heavyweights, and Super Heavyweights.

FOOD AND ACTIVITY RECORD

NAME: _____   _____ I EXERCISED FOR _____ CONSECUTIVE MINUTES
                                    _____ I DID NOT EXERCISE

DATE	TIME	FOOD	AMOUNT	PLACE	HUNGER (0-5)	MOOD

FOOD AND ACTIVITY RECORD

NAME: _____   _____ I EXERCISED FOR _____ CONSECUTIVE MINUTES

_____ I DID NOT EXERCISE

DATE	TIME	FOOD	AMOUNT	PLACE	HUNGER (0-5)	MOOD

FOOD AND ACTIVITY RECORD

NAME: _____   _____ I EXERCISED FOR _____ CONSECUTIVE MINUTES

                                         _____ I DID NOT EXERCISE

DATE	TIME	FOOD	AMOUNT	PLACE	HUNGER (0-5)	MOOD

ABSTINENCE IN ACTION

FOOD AND ACTIVITY RECORD

NAME: _____   _____ I EXERCISED FOR _____ CONSECUTIVE MINUTES

_____ I DID NOT EXERCISE

DATE	TIME	FOOD	AMOUNT	PLACE	HUNGER (0-5)	MOOD

FOOD AND ACTIVITY RECORD

NAME: _____   _____ I EXERCISED FOR _____ CONSECUTIVE MINUTES

_____ I DID NOT EXERCISE

DATE	TIME	FOOD	AMOUNT	PLACE	HUNGER (0-5)	MOOD

FOOD AND ACTIVITY RECORD

NAME: _____   _____ I EXERCISED FOR _____ CONSECUTIVE MINUTES

_____ I DID NOT EXERCISE

DATE	TIME	FOOD	AMOUNT	PLACE	HUNGER (0-5)	MOOD

FOOD AND ACTIVITY RECORD

NAME: _____   _____ I EXERCISED FOR _____ CONSECUTIVE MINUTES

_____ I DID NOT EXERCISE

DATE	TIME	FOOD	AMOUNT	PLACE	HUNGER (0-5)	MOOD

Chapter 6

Eating Away from Home

Advantages and disadvantages of fast-food eating are recognized by some nutritionists. While we may think they are opposed to fast food, they do see the advantages. Chief among these is that fast foods provide us with plenty of protein: up to 50 to 100 percent of our daily need, depending on our selections. Likewise, one fast-food meal may supply us with 30 to 60 percent of our body's requirement of iron and calcium. A beef sandwich plus a milk shake fulfills this order.

Other advantages are that fast food is affordable for many. And, of course, it is fast. Most of us can afford the occasional treat of eating in this manner, especially since no tip is required. Since we're often on the run, eliminating meal preparation time is a definite plus. The locations of fast-food restaurants are convenient.

Nevertheless, fast food is usually oozing with calories, due to the high fat content. Most fast foods are fried, which is the main source of fat. They're also high in sodium. Unless a trip to the salad bar is included, the meal is likely to be low in vitamins A and C and fiber. Finally, unless cheese, milk, or milk shakes are included, we come up short in calcium.

Refer to Table XII (Is Fast Food Fat Food?) on page 79 to understand how to interpret the fat content of fast food. Keep in mind that Table XII is not meant to be an exclusive listing of all fast-food items. Once you know how to decipher the information in this table, however, you'll be able to evaluate the fat data listed in a brochure prepared by fast-food chains regarding its foods.

For example, look in the column marked "Fat (grams)" for McDonald's Big Mac (under the Specialty Burgers section). Notice that there are 36 grams of fat in this sandwich. Since 36 grams is a difficult quantity to comprehend, let's take that 36 grams and translate it into a more recognizable figure. Since there are 4 grams of fat in a teaspoon of margarine, butter, or oil, we need to divide 36 grams of fat by 4 to determine the number of teaspoons of fat in a Big Mac. Hence, there are 9 teaspoons of butter, margarine, or oil according to the "Fat (tsp.)" column for the Big Mac. Eating a Big Mac is like eating 9 teaspoons of butter, margarine, or oil!

Next, let's figure the percentage of calories in the Big Mac that come from fat. Since there are 9 calories in every gram of fat, we need to multiply 36 grams by 9 calories. Three hundred twenty-four of the 570 calories in the Big Mac are in the form of fat. If you divide the 324 calories by the 570 total calories in the Big Mac, this tells you that 57 percent (over half) of the calories in the sandwich come from fat (see the "Fat (percent)" column in Table XII).

We don't want you to become compulsive about calculating and translating the fat information for fast foods. Constant calculating can be destructive to your recovery plan. If you frequently eat at fast-food restaurants, you need to be somewhat knowledgeable about these foods if you expect to maintain your physical abstinence recovery plan.

For example, you may think a chicken sandwich would be a better choice than a hamburger, but this is not usually true at a fast-food restaurant. Refer to Table XII and notice that a Chicken Littles sandwich from Kentucky Fried Chicken is 46 percent fat; a hamburger from Hardee's is only 33 percent fat. Due to a lower fat percentage, a hamburger is sometimes a better selection than a chicken sandwich. Remember, the Abstinence in Action Recovery Plan's emphasis is not on calories, but the reduction of your intake of fat.

We do encourage you to ask or write for nutritional information of your favorite fast foods. The addresses of fast-food restaurants are listed at the end of this chapter. You can ask your local fast-food restaurants for information regarding the content of their foods.

TABLE XII
IS FAST FOOD FAT FOOD?

SANDWICHES	Approximate Calories	Approximate Fat (grams)	Approximate Fat (tsp.)	Approximate Fat (Percent)
Hamburgers				
Hardee's	244	9	2¼	33
McDonald's	260	12	3	42
Cheeseburgers				
Hardee's	327	15	3¾	41
McDonald's	320	16	4	45
Specialty Burgers				
Hardee's Big Deluxe	503	29	7¼	52
McDonald's Big Mac	570	36	9	57
Roast Beef				
Hardee's (Regular)	312	12	3	35
Hardee's (Big)	440	22	5½	45
Chicken				
Hardee's Chicken Fillet	446	17	4¼	34
Kentucky Fried Chicken (Chicken Littles Sandwich)	174	9	2¼	46
McNuggets (6)	320	20	5	56
Fish				
Hardee's Fisherman's Fillet	469	20	5	38
McDonald's	430	26	6½	54
POTATOES				
Fries (regular)				
Hardee's	252	12	3	43
McDonald's	220	10	2½	41
Kentucky Fried Chicken Fries	268	13	3¼	44

This information is provided by
the restaurants listed above.

Restaurant Dining Tips

Cocktails and appetizers can quickly send your calorie tab skyrocketing. Try limiting yourself to one alcoholic beverage or a nonalcoholic drink such as mineral water with a twist of lemon or lime. Wise appetizer selections include fruit or vegetable juice, fresh vegetables (easy on the dip!), clear broth soups, or fresh shrimp.

For protein, select meat, fish, chicken, or turkey that has been roasted, broiled, or baked instead of fried. This will help you eliminate extra fat and calories. Chicken, turkey, and fish are low in fat; removing the skin (a hidden source of fat) will eliminate extra calories. If you prefer red meat, beef round, flank steak, or filet mignon will be your leanest choice (if you trim away visible fat).

Limit butter, gravy, and cream sauces loaded with fat and calories. Baked potatoes and steamed or salad vegetables will help keep your meals on the "lite" side. If you are full or don't need to eat everything that comes with your meal, ask to take the leftovers home, or try ordering a la carte next time.

Ask the Waiter

1. Request salad dressing on the side. This will save you and your salad from drowning in excess fat and calories.
2. Are cream sauces, butter, or gravy added to menu items after cooking? Ordering without these extras can open up a whole new variety of lean menu options.
3. Requesting butter and sour cream on the side gives you control over fat and calories.
4. Some restaurants make half-portions available. Such an option can save you from the temptation to overindulge.
5. Ask to have your fish broiled without butter or margarine.
6. Is fruit listed as an appetizer? It also makes a great dessert substitute.

Using the information on the previous page as a guide, circle the restaurant menu items in Table XIII that would be moderate to low in fat. Put a check mark next to items that you think require questions of the waiter. Checked items would need to be questioned for any of these reasons:

- you're uncertain how the item is prepared or served based on the description given;
- you're uncertain whether the menu item is available with low-fat preparation; and
- you're uncertain of the cut of meat or type of fish being served.
- Compare your responses against those identified in the answer key.

TABLE XIII
RESTAURANT USA MENU

APPETIZERS

Shrimp Cocktail	Fresh Fruit Cup	Hot Soup of the Day
Chilled Fruit Juice	Chilled Tomato Juice	Mock Turtle Soup

ENTREES

Creamed Chicken and Biscuits	New York Strip Steak
Specialty Fried Chicken	Filet Mignon
Pan Fried Boneless Pork Chops	Steak and Lobster
Baked Sugar Cured Ham	Broiled Scallops
Marinated Boneless Chicken Breast	Seafood Combo

VEGETABLES

Baked Potato	Vegetable of the Day
Mashed Potatoes with Gravy	Tossed Salad
Salad Bar	

DESSERTS

Cheesecake	Ice Cream	Apple Pie

Compare your responses against those identified in the answer key below.

TABLE XIV
RESTAURANT USA MENU

APPETIZERS

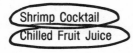 Shrimp Cocktail   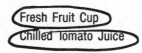 Fresh Fruit Cup   ✓Hot Soup of the Day

Chilled Fruit Juice   Chilled Tomato Juice   ✓Mock Turtle Soup

ENTREES

Creamed Chicken and Biscuits   New York Strip Steak

Specialty Fried Chicken   ✓Filet Mignon

Pan Fried Boneless Pork Chops   ✓Steak and Lobster

✓Baked Sugar Cured Ham   ✓Broiled Scallops

✓Marinated Boneless Chicken Breast   ✓Seafood Combo

VEGETABLES

✓Baked Potato   ✓Vegetable of the Day

Mashed Potatoes with Gravy   ✓Tossed Salad

✓Salad Bar

DESSERTS

Cheesecake   Ice Cream   Apple Pie

If you want dining out to be pleasurable, an all-or-nothing philosophy will leave you feeling deprived; consequently, you might want to go home and eat something you *really* want, possibly binging. The following meal is a good example of how you could set yourself up for such a compulsive eating episode:

Broiled Fish — no butter or margarine.
Baked Potato — no butter or margarine.
Tossed Salad — with lemon juice.
Fresh Fruit
Iced Tea — with Sweet-N-Low.

Remember, the idea is to *limit* your eating of high-fat foods, not make yourself feel persecuted. To revise this dinner menu so that it is more exciting to the taste buds and less likely to leave you feeling deprived, you might choose the following:

Broiled Fish — tartar sauce or cocktail sauce on the side.
Baked Potato — butter, margarine, or sour cream on the side.
(Use 50 to 75 percent of your usual portion.)
Tossed Salad — with salad dressing on the side.
(Again, use 50 to 75 percent of your usual portion.)
Fresh fruit — or split a dessert with a friend.
Iced Tea — with Sweet-N-Low.

Don't hesitate to ask for dressings, butter, margarine, or sauces on the side. Most restaurants are more than willing to accommodate such requests; they want your business. You'll be much happier because you can choose how much fat will be topping your meal. You're taking an active step toward developing a comfortable relationship with food.

Commitment Contract Review

Review your food and activity records from the past week to determine whether you achieved your Commitment Contract goals. Remember to reward yourself if you met your goals. If you didn't meet the goals, evaluate why. Were the goals too difficult or unrealistic? How could the goals have been designed to be more achievable?

Commitment Contract: Upcoming Week

Use Table XV on the next page to plan a Commitment Contract for the next seven days. If you met your Commitment Contract goals for this past week, continue to include them on this week's contract.

Instead of adding a new goal to your Commitment Contract this week, focus on increasing the *frequency* of your current goals. For example, compare Jill Smith's Commitment Contract in Table XI on page 68 against her contract in Table XVI on page 86. Notice for goal "1" that Jill increased the number of days she will limit herself to eating three to four times per day from two to three days per week to three to four days per week. In addition, she increased the days for goal "2" from two to three days to three to four days. Since Jill increased the frequency of her two food goals, she decided to keep her exercise activity goal the same. You may choose to increase the frequency of your exercise goals and one food goal.

TABLE XV
COMMITMENT CONTRACT

Name: _____

Period of Contract: From _____ to _____

1. What is my goal?

My goal is: _____

_____

_____

_____

_____

2. What is my reward?

If I achieve my goal, I may: _____

_____

_____

3. If I do not achieve my goal, I agree that I will not receive my reward.

Signed: _____

Date: _____

4. I achieved my goal for this contract.

_____ Yes

_____ No, explain: _____

_____

_____

TABLE XVI
SAMPLE COMMITMENT CONTRACT

Name: _____*Jill Smith*_____

Period of Contract: From ___*Dec. 8*___ to ___*December 15*___

1. What is my goal?

My goal is: *(1) 3 to 4 days out of the next week I will limit myself to eating 3 to 4 times per day. (2) 3 to 4 days out of the next week I will limit myself to 2 to 3 high-fat foods (Heavy & Super Heavy weights) (3) I will walk for 15 consecutive minutes 3 days out of the next week and I will monitor my heart to my working heart rate level each time.*

2. What is my reward?

If I achieve my goal, I may: *Call a friend long distance and talk for 30 minutes.*

3. If I do not achieve my goal, I agree that I will not receive my reward.

Signed: _____*Jill Smith*_____

Date: _____*December 8*_____

4. I achieved my goal for this contract.

_____ Yes

_____ No, explain: _____

_____

Assignment

1. Fill out Food and Activity Records (on the following pages) each day for the next seven days.

2. Focus on fulfilling the food and exercise goals you chose for the upcoming week on your Commitment Contract.

3. Go to a favorite restaurant (not fast food) and request a menu. Practice making meal selections that are low to moderate in fat (including an appetizer, entree, vegetables — dessert is optional).

4. Wait seven days before proceeding to Chapter Seven.

Fast-Food Restaurant Corporate Headquarter Addresses

ARBY'S
AFA Service Corporation
Suite 700/Ten Piedmont Center
3495 Piedmont Road, N.E.
Atlanta, GA 30305

ARTHUR TREACHER'S FISH AND CHIPS
4959 Mahoning Avenue
Youngstown, OH 44515

BURGER KING CORPORATION
Consumer Information M/S 1441
P.O. Box 520783
Miami, FL 33152

CHURCH'S FRIED CHICKEN, INC.
P.O. Box BH001
San Antonio, TX 78284

D'LITES OF AMERICA, INC.
6075 The Corners Parkway
Suite 200
Norcross, GA 30092

HARDEE'S FOOD SYSTEMS
Menu Development Department
1233 N. Church Street
Rocky Mount, NC 27801

INTERNATIONAL DAIRY QUEEN, INC.
P.O. Box 35286
Minneapolis, MN 55435

JACK IN THE BOX
Foodmakers, Inc.
9330 Balboa Avenue
San Diego, CA 92123

KENTUCKY FRIED CHICKEN
Public Affairs Department
P.O. Box 32070
Louisville, KY 40232

LONG JOHN SILVER'S
Jerrico, Inc.
P.O. Box 11988
Lexington, KY 40579

MCDONALD'S CORPORATION
Consumer Affairs
McDonald's Plaza
Oak Brook, IL 60521

PIZZA HUT, INC.
Consumer Affairs Department
P.O. Box 428
Wichita, KS 67201

ROY ROGERS RESTAURANTS
Marriott Corporation
Marriott Drive
Washington, D.C. 20058

TACO BELL
16808 Armstong Avenue
Irvine, CA 92714

WENDY'S INTERNATIONAL, INC.
Consumer Affairs Department
P.O. Box 256
Dublin, OH 43017

Contact your local chapter of the American Heart Association, and ask if they have a guide regarding menu recommendations (items that are low to moderate in fat) for your area's restaurants.

FOOD AND ACTIVITY RECORD

NAME: _____   _____ I EXERCISED FOR _____ CONSECUTIVE MINUTES
                                         _____ I DID NOT EXERCISE

DATE	TIME	FOOD	AMOUNT	PLACE	HUNGER (0-5)	MOOD

FOOD AND ACTIVITY RECORD

NAME: _____   _____ I EXERCISED FOR _____ CONSECUTIVE MINUTES

_____ I DID NOT EXERCISE

DATE	TIME	FOOD	AMOUNT	PLACE	HUNGER (0-5)	MOOD

FOOD AND ACTIVITY RECORD

NAME: _____   _____ I EXERCISED FOR _____ CONSECUTIVE MINUTES

_____ I DID NOT EXERCISE

DATE	TIME	FOOD	AMOUNT	PLACE	HUNGER (0-5)	MOOD

FOOD AND ACTIVITY RECORD

NAME: _____   _____ I EXERCISED FOR _____ CONSECUTIVE MINUTES
                                    _____ I DID NOT EXERCISE

DATE	TIME	FOOD	AMOUNT	PLACE	HUNGER (0-5)	MOOD

ABSTINENCE IN ACTION

FOOD AND ACTIVITY RECORD

NAME: _____   _____ I EXERCISED FOR _____ CONSECUTIVE MINUTES

_____ I DID NOT EXERCISE

DATE	TIME	FOOD	AMOUNT	PLACE	HUNGER (0-5)	MOOD

FOOD AND ACTIVITY RECORD

NAME: _____   _____ I EXERCISED FOR _____ CONSECUTIVE MINUTES

_____ I DID NOT EXERCISE

DATE	TIME	FOOD	AMOUNT	PLACE	HUNGER (0-5)	MOOD

ABSTINENCE IN ACTION

FOOD AND ACTIVITY RECORD

NAME: _____   _____ I EXERCISED FOR _____ CONSECUTIVE MINUTES

_____ I DID NOT EXERCISE

DATE	TIME	FOOD	AMOUNT	PLACE	HUNGER (0-5)	MOOD

Chapter 7

Putting It All Together: Part I

In last week's chapter, Eating Away from Home, we identified the advantages and disadvantages of eating at restaurants.

In this chapter, you'll begin putting together the framework of your food and exercise plan.

The first step in designing your personalized food and recovery plan is to review the following materials:

- Your scores on the Compulsive Eater's Behavior Inventory (see Chapter One).
- The program's Abstinence in Action Recovery Plan (outlined in Chapter One).
- Your Food and Activity Records from the past four weeks.
- Your Commitment Contracts from the past four weeks.

Remember, low scores on the Compulsive Eater's Behavior Inventory indicate behaviors linked to compulsive eating; high scores indicate behaviors associated with recovery from compulsive eating. Consequently, the categories in which you have low scores are important ones to include in your food and exercise plan.

The Abstinence in Action Recovery Plan will guide you on how to change your relationship with food and your food behaviors in your recovery program. Your food and activity records and commitment contracts from the past four weeks will give you firsthand evidence of your success so far in changing your relationship with food, your food behaviors, and your exercise habits.

Now that you have reviewed the material at the beginning of this chapter, use Table XVII (My Personal Food and Exercise Recovery Plan) beginning on page 99 to begin designing your recovery plan. Table XVIII gives an example of how a person might complete the first draft of her or his recovery plan. Please keep this in mind: your plan is flexible, not cast in stone. If you find that part of it doesn't work or becomes outdated, you may wish to change it. But the more realistic you are now in designing your recovery plan, the less change will be necessary later on.

Assignment

1. Fill out Food and Activity Records (see pages 105-111) each day for the next seven days.

2. Focus on meeting the food and exercise goals you chose for yourself on your Personal Food and Exercise Recovery Plan. Choose a reward that you'll give yourself if you meet your goals by the end of the next week.

3. Wait seven days before reading Chapter Eight.

TABLE XVII
MY PERSONAL FOOD AND
EXERCISE RECOVERY PLAN

I. FOOD RELATIONSHIPS AND BEHAVIORS

1. Meal Timing/Frequency

My goal is to: _____

_____

_____

_____

2. Binge Foods (sweets and foods high in fat)

My goal is to: _____

_____

_____

_____

3. Binging

My goal is to: _____

_____

_____

_____

4. Environment and Feelings

My goal is to: _____

_____

_____

_____

TABLE XVII
MY PERSONAL FOOD AND
<u>EXERCISE RECOVERY PLAN</u> (Continued)

II. FOOD STRATEGY GUIDELINE

My goal is to: _____

_____

_____

_____

Meal #1 (Time: _____)

Protein _____

Dairy _____

Grain
Bread/Starch _____

Fruit/Vegetable _____

Beverage _____

Other/Fats _____

Meal #2 (Time: _____)

Protein _____

Dairy _____

Grain
Bread/Starch _____

Fruit/Vegetable _____

Beverage _____

Other/Fats _____

TABLE XVII
MY PERSONAL FOOD AND
<u>EXERCISE RECOVERY PLAN</u> (Continued)

Meal #3 (Time: _____)

Protein _____

Dairy _____

Grain
Bread/Starch _____

Fruit/Vegetable _____

Beverage _____

Other/Fats _____

III. EXERCISE/ACTIVITY

My goal is to: _____

_____

_____

_____

TABLE XVIII
(SAMPLE)
MY PERSONAL FOOD AND
EXERCISE RECOVERY PLAN

I. FOOD RELATIONSHIPS AND BEHAVIORS

1. Meal Timing/Frequency

My goal is to: *(1) I will continue to limit myself to eating 3 to 4 times per day for 3 to 4 days out of each week since I have had success with this goal on my past commitment contracts. (2) I am ready to start eating a breakfast meal at least 2 to 3 days per week.*

2. Binge Foods (sweets and foods high in fat)

My goal is to: *I will continue to limit myself to a total of 2 to 3 high-fat foods (Heavy & Super Heavy-weights) 3 to 4 days out of each week since I have had success with this goal on my past commitment contracts.*

3. Binging

My goal is to: *This is a tough area for me. The best I can do for right now is to limit weighing myself to one time per day since I'm used to weighing myself 3 times a day.*

4. Environment and Feelings

My goal is to: *I am not ready to tackle this area yet. I will focus my efforts on my other goals right now.*

ABSTINENCE IN ACTION

TABLE XVIII
(SAMPLE)
MY PERSONAL FOOD AND
EXERCISE RECOVERY PLAN
(Continued)

II. FOOD STRATEGY GUIDELINE

My goal is to: *(1) start eating breakfast sometime between 6 and 7 a.m., 2 to 3 days per week according to the plan I have designed (2) For meals #2 and #3, I will focus on eating them at the designated times and cut down on fat intake.*

Meal #1 (Time: *6 to 7 am* **)**

Protein *Optional - 1 ounce*

Dairy *8 ounces of 2% milk or an 8 ounce cup of non-fruit yogurt*

Grain
Bread/Starch *2 servings (1 whole bagel, or 2 slices toast, or 1 ounce cereal & 1 slice toast)*

Fruit/Vegetable *1 medium piece of any kind of fruit*

Beverage *Calorie-free*

Other/Fats *50% of my usual intake*

Meal #2 (Time: *12 to 1* **)**

Protein _____

Dairy _____

Grain
Bread/Starch _____

Fruit/Vegetable _____

Beverage _____

Other/Fats *50% of my usual intake*

TABLE XVIII
(SAMPLE)
**MY PERSONAL FOOD AND
EXERCISE RECOVERY PLAN**
(Continued)

Meal #3 (Time: _5:30 - 6:30_

Protein _____

Dairy _____

Grain
Bread/Starch _____

Fruit/Vegetable _____

Beverage _____

Other/Fats _50% of my usual intake_____

III. EXERCISE/ACTIVITY

My goal is to: _do some type of exercise (especially walking or riding my stationary bike) that will raise my heart rate to my working heart rate level for 3 days each week & for 15 to 20 consecutive minutes each day._

FOOD AND ACTIVITY RECORD

NAME: _____   _____ I EXERCISED FOR _____ CONSECUTIVE MINUTES

_____ I DID NOT EXERCISE

DATE	TIME	FOOD	AMOUNT	PLACE	HUNGER (0-5)	MOOD

FOOD AND ACTIVITY RECORD

NAME: _____ _____ I EXERCISED FOR _____ CONSECUTIVE MINUTES

_____ I DID NOT EXERCISE

DATE	TIME	FOOD	AMOUNT	PLACE	HUNGER (0-5)	MOOD

FOOD AND ACTIVITY RECORD

NAME: _____ _____ I EXERCISED FOR _____ CONSECUTIVE MINUTES

_____ I DID NOT EXERCISE

DATE	TIME	FOOD	AMOUNT	PLACE	HUNGER (0-5)	MOOD

FOOD AND ACTIVITY RECORD

NAME: _____   _____ I EXERCISED FOR _____ CONSECUTIVE MINUTES

_____ I DID NOT EXERCISE

DATE	TIME	FOOD	AMOUNT	PLACE	HUNGER (0-5)	MOOD

ABSTINENCE IN ACTION

FOOD AND ACTIVITY RECORD

NAME: _____   _____ I EXERCISED FOR _____ CONSECUTIVE MINUTES

_____ I DID NOT EXERCISE

DATE	TIME	FOOD	AMOUNT	PLACE	HUNGER (0-5)	MOOD

FOOD AND ACTIVITY RECORD

NAME: _____   _____ I EXERCISED FOR _____ CONSECUTIVE MINUTES

_____ I DID NOT EXERCISE

DATE	TIME	FOOD	AMOUNT	PLACE	HUNGER (0-5)	MOOD

ABSTINENCE IN ACTION

FOOD AND ACTIVITY RECORD

NAME: _____

_____ I EXERCISED FOR _____ CONSECUTIVE MINUTES

_____ I DID NOT EXERCISE

DATE	TIME	FOOD	AMOUNT	PLACE	HUNGER (0-5)	MOOD

Chapter 8

Trim the Fat: Part II

This week's chapter is devoted to completing specific, practical food activities that will help you continue to reduce your intake of foods high in fat. Since reducing fat from your menu has been so emphasized, you might have the impression that fat is all bad. But fat does offer the following benefits.

- Fat serves as a source of energy.
- Fat provides flavor and satisfies the appetite.
- Fat helps vitamins A, D, E, and K to be absorbed.
- Fat keeps your skin in good condition.

As a part of your body weight, fat:

- protects vital body organs from being harmed during a fall or accident,
- provides the body with insulation to protect it from drastic temperature changes in your environment,
- serves as a storehouse of energy for the body, and
- provides part of the structure of every body cell.

Fat has some valuable contributions to offer to our comfort, health, and enjoyment of life. The problem is not fat itself — it's the amount eaten. While the level recommended by most nutrition and health experts is 30 percent, the average American eats about 40 percent of daily calories in the form of fat.

As you may recall from Chapter Five, there are several major benefits of reducing your fat intake:

- reducing your calorie intake fairly quickly,

- encouraging your body to lower its set point weight,
- causing more calories to be burned in your body,
- decreasing, maybe, your risk of certain types of cancer, and
- reducing your risk of heart disease.

How do people reduce their fat intake to 30 percent or less so that they can enjoy the benefits we've just reviewed? The following activities will help answer this question.

Fat Finding Activity

Review the Getting to Know Your Fat Worksheet: Answer Key on page 62 and the Trimming Fat and Refined Sugar information on pages 63-65, and identify those foods and beverages on the Fat Finding Activity worksheet in Table XIX (page 115) which are high in fat. Specifically, foods high in fat would be those that fall into the Heavyweight and Super Heavyweight categories.

Circle the foods and beverages on Table XIX that are high in fat. When you've finished, go back to each of these items and write recommendations for modifying the foods and beverages or make substitutions that will help reduce the fat content of the day's meals. When you're finished, compare your responses against those in Answer Keys I and II on Tables XX (page 116) and XXI (page 117).

TABLE XIX
FAT FINDING ACTIVITY

NAME: _____

DATE	TIME	FOOD	AMOUNT	PLACE	HUNGER (0-5)	MOOD
5/26	8:00 a.m.	coffee, cream	1 cup 1 tbsp			
		Whole wheat toast	2 slices			
		Butter	1 tbsp			
	10:00 a.m.	Fresh orange	1 medium			
	12 noon	Bologna & American cheese	1 oz bologna 1 oz slice cheese			
		sandwich with mayo Tossed salad (lettuce,	2 slices ww bread, 2 tbsp mayo, 1 cup lettuce			
		green pepper, carrots, onions, cherry tomatoes,	(2 tbsp each) 3 tomatoes			
		sunflower seeds, Thousand Island dressing)	2 tbsp 4 tbsp			
		Diet cola	12 oz			
	4:30 p.m.	Whole milk	8 oz			
		Chocolate chip cookies	3			
	6:00 p.m.	Plain T-Bone steak	8 oz			
		Baked potato	1 medium			
		Sour cream Butter	1 tbsp 1 tbsp			
		Green beans	½ cup			
		Bacon	1 strip			
		Chocolate Ice Cream	1 cup			
	10:00 p.m.	M&M's (Peanut)	1.67 oz bag			

TABLE XX
FAT FINDING ACTIVITY: ANSWER KEY I
(FOODS HIGH IN FAT)

NAME: _Jill Smith_

DATE	TIME	FOOD	AMOUNT	PLACE	HUNGER (0-5)	MOOD
5/26	8:00 a.m.	coffee, (cream)	1 cup 1 tbsp			
		Whole wheat toast	2 slices			
		(Butter)	1 tbsp			
	10:00 a.m.	Fresh orange	1 medium			
	12 noon	(Bologna & American cheese sandwich with mayo)	1 oz bologna 1 oz slice cheese 2 slices ww bread, 2 tbsp mayo,			
		Tossed salad (lettuce, green pepper, carrots, onions, cherry tomatoes,	1 cup lettuce (2 tbsp each) 3 tomatoes			
		(sunflower seeds,) (Thousand Island dressing)	2 tbsp 4 tbsp			
		Diet cola	12 oz			
	4:30 p.m.	(Whole milk)	8 oz			
		(Chocolate chip cookies)	3			
	6:00 p.m.	(Plain T-Bone steak)	8 oz			
		Baked potato	1 medium			
		(Sour cream)	1 tbsp			
		(Butter)	1 tbsp			
		Green beans	½ cup			
		(Bacon)	1 strip			
		(Chocolate Ice Cream)	1 cup			
	10:00 p.m.	(M&M's (Peanut))	1.67 oz bag			

TABLE XXI

FAT FINDING ACTIVITY: ANSWER KEY II
(FAT REDUCTION RECOMMENDATIONS)

NAME: _____

DATE	TIME	FOOD	AMOUNT	PLACE	HUNGER (0-5)	MOOD
5/26	8:00 a.m.	Coffee Cream, Whole Milk, 2%, or Half & Half	1 cup Reduce to 1 to 2 tsps.			
		Whole Wheat Toast	2 slices			
		Butter	Reduce to 1-1½ tsp (Using margarine is to your advantage for lowering cholesterol and saturated fat and providing essential fat to keep your skin in good condition.)			
	10:00 a.m.	Fresh Orange	1 medium			
	12 noon	Turkey & Borden	1 oz turkey 1 oz slice cheese			
		Lite-Line American Cheese	2 slices ww bread			
		Sandwich	1 tbsp Miracle Whip Lite or Weight Watchers			
			Reduced Calorie Mayonnaise, or another brand or 1½ tsp regular mayonnaise			
		Tossed salad (lettuce,	1 cup			
		green pepper, carrots, onions cherry tomatoes)	2 tbsp each 3			
		Sunflower seeds	Reduce to 1 or ½ tbsp			
		Thousand Island Dressing	Reduce to 2 tbsp. or use 2 to 3 tbsp reduced calorie Thousand Island Dressing			
		Diet Cola	12 oz.			
	4:30 p.m.	Toasted bagel	½			
		Margarine	1 tsp or 1 tbsp cream cheese or 1 tbsp low-fat cream cheese			
		2%, 1%, or skim milk	8 oz			
	6:00 p.m.	Plain T-Bone Steak	Reduce to (Also possible to switch to 4 oz chicken or fish)			
		Baked potato Sour cream & butter	1 medium 1 to 2 tsp each or 1 tbsp of butter or sour cream, but not both.			
		Green beans Bacon	½ cup ½ strip (½ strip bacon has about the same calories as ½ tsp butter or margarine. Margarine has no cholesterol and is lower in saturated fat.)			
		Chocolate Ice Cream	Reduce to ½ cup or substitute ice milk or fresh fruit in season.			
	10:00 p.m.	M&M's (Peanut)	Reduce to ½ bag or substitute 1 piece fresh fruit in season. Work toward deleting snacks this late in the evening.			

Thus far you have had the opportunity to get better acquainted with the fat content of various foods by reviewing a day's meals and snacks for foods high in fat. In addition, you made modifications or substitutions to reduce the day's fat intake. Both of these activities involved the use of the Trimming Fat and Refined Sugar information plus the Getting To Know Your Fat Worksheet: Answer Key.

Another way to identify the fat content of various foods and beverages is to evaluate food labels by calculating (1) the number of calories in one serving of a product that come from fat, and (2) the percent of total calories in one serving of a product that come from fat. Using the Sample Product Label below, let's try these calculations.

SAMPLE PRODUCT

Nutrition Information Per Serving

Serving Size ...... 1 oz. (approx. 1 cup)
Servings per container . . 4
Calories 130
Protein . . . . 5 grams
Carbohydrate . . . 16 grams
Fat . . . . 5 grams

In order to translate the gram information for fat into calories, you need to know that fat has nine calories per gram. Now, to determine the number of fat calories in one serving of the Sample Product, multiply the grams of fat listed on the food label by the calories per gram of fat. Let's figure this out together:

- Five grams of fat in one serving of the Sample Product × 9 calories per gram of fat = 45 fat calories in one serving of the Sample Product.

By knowing the number of fat calories in one serving of the Sample Product (45 calories), and by knowing the total number of calories in one serving of the Sample Product (130 calories), we can now calculate the percent of total calories in one serving of the Sample Product that come from fat. We need to divide the fat calories in one serving of the Sample Product by the total number of calories in one serving of the Sample Product. Then multiply the answer by 100 to figure the percent.

- Forty-five calories from fat in one serving of the Sample Product divided by 130 total calories in one serving of the Sample Product = .35, and .35 × 100 = 35 percent of the calories in one serving of the Sample Product come from fat.

There is one other way of evaluating the fat content of food items, using food labels. This process involves translating the grams of fat in one serving of a food product into teaspoon equivalents. In other words, how many teaspoons of pure fat (butter, margarine, or oil) are contained in one serving of the product?

In order to translate the gram information for fat into teaspoon equivalents, you need to know that there are four grams of fat in a teaspoon of a pure fat source such as butter, margarine, or oil. To determine the teaspoon equivalents of fat in one serving of the Sample Product, divide the grams of fat in one serving of the Sample Product by the grams of fat in a teaspoon of a pure fat source. Let's calculate the teaspoon equivalents of fat contained in one serving of the Sample Product.

- Five grams of fat in one serving of the Sample Product divided by four grams of fat in one teaspoon of a pure fat source equals 1¼ teaspoons of fat in one serving of the Sample Product. Therefore, eating one serving of the Sample Product means that you will be eating the amount of fat you would find in 1¼ teaspoons margarine, oil, or butter.

You now have the knowledge to interpret food labels to determine the percent of calories derived from fat and to translate the grams of fat into teaspoon equivalents. This knowledge will be valuable when evaluating new products on the market or foods that do not appear on the Trimming Fat and Refined Sugar section of Chapter Five.

Food and Exercise Recovery Plan Review

Last week you completed your first draft of your Food and Exercise Recovery Plan. If you fulfilled your goals, don't forget to follow through with your reward. If you had a difficult time or didn't meet your goals, evaluate why and adjust your goals on your recovery plan to be more realistic.

Commitment Contract: Upcoming Week

Use the Commitment Contract in Table XXII on the next page to set your goals for the next week. We recommend that you continue to work on the goals you have already established for yourself on the first draft of your food and exercise plan (of course, you can revise your goals if they didn't work out). Since you have only been working on your plan for one week, we suggest that you do not add any new goals to your Commitment Contract this week. Refer to Table XXIII on page 121 for an example of how to complete this week's contract.

TABLE XXII

COMMITMENT CONTRACT

Name: _____

Period of Contract: From _____ to _____

1. What is my goal?

My goal is: _____

_____

_____

_____

_____

2. What is my reward?

If I achieve my goal, I may: _____

_____

_____

3. If I do not achieve my goal, I agree that I will not receive my reward.

Signed: _____

Date: _____

4. I achieved my goal for this contract.

_____ Yes

_____ No, explain: _____

_____

_____

TABLE XXIII
SAMPLE COMMITMENT CONTRACT

Name: _Jill Smith_

Period of Contract: From _January 2_ to _January 9_

1. What is my goal?

My goal is: _to continue following my goals as designated on the first draft of my food and exercise recovery plan._

2. What is my reward?

If I achieve my goal, I may: _get a babysitter to watch the kids while I go out shopping for 2 or 3 hours._

3. If I do not achieve my goal, I agree that I will not receive my reward.

Signed: _Jill Smith_

Date: _January 2_

4. I achieved my goal for this contract.

_____ Yes

_____ No, explain: _____

Assignment

1. Fill out Food and Activity Records (on the following pages) each day for the next seven days.

2. Focus on achieving the food and exercise goals you have identified on the first draft of your Food and Exercise Recovery Plan.

3. Use the nutrition labels on two or three food packages that you have around the house to practice calculating the percent of calories derived from fat and translating the grams of fat into teaspoon equivalents.

4. Wait seven days before reading Chapter Nine.

FOOD AND ACTIVITY RECORD

NAME: _____   _____ I EXERCISED FOR _____ CONSECUTIVE MINUTES

_____ I DID NOT EXERCISE

DATE	TIME	FOOD	AMOUNT	PLACE	HUNGER (0-5)	MOOD

FOOD AND ACTIVITY RECORD

NAME: _____   _____ I EXERCISED FOR _____ CONSECUTIVE MINUTES

_____ I DID NOT EXERCISE

DATE	TIME	FOOD	AMOUNT	PLACE	HUNGER (0-5)	MOOD

ABSTINENCE IN ACTION

FOOD AND ACTIVITY RECORD

NAME: _____   _____ I EXERCISED FOR _____ CONSECUTIVE MINUTES
_____ I DID NOT EXERCISE

DATE	TIME	FOOD	AMOUNT	PLACE	HUNGER (0-5)	MOOD

FOOD AND ACTIVITY RECORD

NAME: _____   _____ I EXERCISED FOR _____ CONSECUTIVE MINUTES

_____ I DID NOT EXERCISE

DATE	TIME	FOOD	AMOUNT	PLACE	HUNGER (0-5)	MOOD

FOOD AND ACTIVITY RECORD

NAME: _____   _____ I EXERCISED FOR _____ CONSECUTIVE MINUTES

_____ I DID NOT EXERCISE

DATE	TIME	FOOD	AMOUNT	PLACE	HUNGER (0-5)	MOOD

FOOD AND ACTIVITY RECORD

NAME: _____   _____ I EXERCISED FOR _____ CONSECUTIVE MINUTES

_____ I DID NOT EXERCISE

DATE	TIME	FOOD	AMOUNT	PLACE	HUNGER (0-5)	MOOD

ABSTINENCE IN ACTION

FOOD AND ACTIVITY RECORD

NAME: _____   _____ I EXERCISED FOR _____ CONSECUTIVE MINUTES

_____ I DID NOT EXERCISE

DATE	TIME	FOOD	AMOUNT	PLACE	HUNGER (0-5)	MOOD

Chapter 9

Eating at Home

It seems that there is less time to devote to food preparation because we have so many obligations at work, school, and with family and friends. What do you do to help ensure that you can prepare a quick, nutritious meal when your schedule doesn't allow time for lengthy preparation? Let's pursue the answer to this question with the following helpful hints:

- Take time to plan ahead.
- Cook meals that last two to three days.
- Use leftovers to make your own frozen dinners.
- Purchase precooked meats and prepare the remaining meal items on your own. (Not all stores have precooked meats, but check the meat market or butcher section of a large supermarket.)
- Buy boneless cuts of meat and fish. These take less time to cook and offer a greater variety of preparation methods.
- Prepare a large bowl of salad fixings (a combination of lettuce, spinach, green pepper, carrots, celery, et cetera) that can be drawn on out of an airtight container for up to three days. Although by the third day the salad won't be as crisp or have as much vitamin or mineral value as the first day or two, the salad will still have food value and is preferable to no vegetables at all.
- Take advantage of appliances such as the food processor or microwave that save preparation and cooking time.
- Store some of the nutritious versions of the new "light" frozen dinners in the freezer section of your refrigerator.

Let's pursue the last recommendation in greater detail. There are criteria that will tell you whether a frozen dinner is not only quick, but also good for your health. To evaluate nutrition labels to determine whether a frozen dinner is quick and nutritious, look for the following information:

- Requires 30 minutes or less preparation time.
- Supplies 300 to 500 calories, or one-third your daily calorie needs.
- Provides 16 grams of protein.
- Contains 1,100 milligrams sodium, or less.
- Supplies 30 percent or less calories from fat.
- Provides 20 percent or greater of the U.S. RDA for two or more of the vitamins or minerals listed.
- Is eaten along with at least another serving of a vegetable and another serving of grain, bread, or starch.

Let's get some practical experience using the criteria just reviewed to evaluate two frozen dinners. Listed below are the nutrition labels from the dinners. Use the Frozen Dinner Evaluation Sheet on page 134 to critique the two dinners.

Frozen Dinner #1: Vegetable Lasagna

Nutrition Information Per Serving

Serving Size	13 oz
Servings per container	1
Calories	280
Protein	24g
Carbohydrate	30g
Fat	7g
Cholesterol	30mg
Sodium	1,100mg
Potassium	700mg

Percentage of U.S. Recommended Daily Allowances (U.S.RDA)

Protein	35	Riboflavin	20
Vitamin A	50	Niacin	10
Vitamin C	30	Calcium	30
Thiamine	10	Iron	6

Cooking Directions: *Conventional Oven* — Heat at 350 degrees for 50 minutes or until hot. *Microwave Oven* — Microwave on high for 10 to 12 minutes.

Frozen Dinner #2: Spaghetti with Meat Sauce

Nutrition Information Per Serving

Serving Size	11 oz
Servings per container	1
Calories	300
Protein	16g
Carbohydrate	42g
Fat	8g

Percentage of U.S. Recommended Daily Allowances (U.S.RDA)

Protein	20	Riboflavin	10
Vitamin A	20	Niacin	20
Vitamin C	15	Calcium	8
Thiamine	15	Iron	30

Cooking Directions: *Range Top* — Drop bags into boiling water and heat for 12 to 14 minutes. *Microwave Oven* — Cut a small slit in center of bags and heat on high for 4 to 6 minutes or until hot.

You need not be compulsive about evaluating every "light" frozen dinner nutrition label at the supermarket. But if you rely on these products for quick meals, it's beneficial to know whether they also are nutritious.

FROZEN DINNER EVALUATION

	Frozen Dinner #1		Frozen Dinner #2	
	Yes	No	Yes	No
1. 30 minutes or less preparation time.	___	___	___	___
2. 300 to 500 calories	___	___	___	___
3. 16 grams protein	___	___	___	___
4. 1,100 mg sodium or less	___	___	___	___
5. 30 percent or less calories from fat*	___	___	___	___
6. 20 percent or greater of the U.S.RDA for two or more of the vitamins or minerals listed	___	___	___	___
7. Overall, do you feel the dinner is quick and nutritious?	___	___	___	___

Comments: _____

_____

_____

_____

*If you've forgotten how to calculate the percentage of calories from fat, then refer to the section in Chapter Eight which reviews this process.

Compare your responses regarding the dinners against the answer key on the following page.

FROZEN DINNER EVALUATION
Answer Key

	Frozen Dinner #1		Frozen Dinner #2	
	Yes	No	Yes	No
1. 30 minutes or less preparation time.	*✓	*✓	✓	—
2. 300 to 500 calories	—	–✓	✓	—
3. 16 grams protein	✓	—	✓	—
4. 1,100 mg sodium or less	✓	—	?	?
5. 30 percent or less calories from fat	✓ (23%)	—	✓ (24%)	—
6. 20 percent or greater of the U.S.RDA for two or more of the vitamins or minerals listed	✓	—	✓	—
7. Overall, do you feel the dinner is quick and nutritious?	✓	—	=✓	=✓

Comments:

* (1) In order for dinner #1 to be quick, you have to use a microwave oven.

– (2) Dinner #1 has only 280 calories. (A standard serving of a vegetable or fruit with the dinner would easily help it meet the 300 calorie minimum recommendation.)

? (4) Sodium information not available for dinner #2.

= (7) Dinner #2 would be quick and nutritious, providing you do not have a blood pressure or heart problem affected by sodium (the sodium information for this dinner isn't available).

We recommended eating a vegetable serving with any of the frozen dinners, along with a serving of bread, grain, or starch.

Fast Food at Home Versus Restaurants

There are both advantages and disadvantages to fixing fast foods at home instead of purchasing fast food at restaurants. What follows are the advantages:

- Better control over the fat content, while your choices at restaurants are limited to items on the menu.
- You have control over the sodium content. Most fast foods are high in sodium, and at restaurants you're at the mercy of the cook.
- Meals fixed at home can be less expensive than eating out.
- Since you're doing the cooking, you can prepare a greater variety of food items, so you may get a greater variety of nutrients, especially compared to many fast-food restaurants.

Here are the disadvantages of cooking fast food at home:

- If you buy high-fat frozen dinners or use much fat in cooking, your home meals could be as high in fat as those purchased at restaurants.
- If you use many canned or convenience products during cooking, your meals may be as high in sodium as those in restaurants. (Remember, several "light" frozen dinners are still high in sodium.)
- Frozen, nutritious dinners from the store can be as expensive as some meals eaten in restaurants.
- Perhaps the major disadvantage of cooking quick, nutritious meals at home is that planning and preparation time are necessary.

Commitment Contract Review

Review your Food and Activity Records from the past week to determine whether your Food and Exercise Recovery Plan is working and realistic for you. Be sure to reward yourself if you met your goals. If you're having difficulty with your goals, adjust or revise them.

Commitment Contract: Upcoming Week

Now use the Commitment Contract in Table XXIV on the next page to design your goals for the next week. Add one additional food-related goal to your contract and evaluate whether or not you're ready to increase your exercise commitment. Refer to Table XXV on page 138 for an example of how to complete this week's contract.

TABLE XXIV
COMMITMENT CONTRACT

Name: _____

Period of Contract: From _____ to _____

1. What is my goal?

My goal is: _____

_____

_____

_____

_____

2. What is my reward?

If I achieve my goal, I may: _____

_____

_____

3. If I do not achieve my goal, I agree that I will not receive my reward.

Signed: _____

Date: _____

4. I achieved my goal for this contract.

_____ Yes

_____ No, explain: _____

_____

_____

TABLE XXV
SAMPLE COMMITMENT CONTRACT

Name: _Jill Smith_

Period of Contract: From _January 9_ to _January 16_

1. What is my goal?

My goal is: _(1) to continue following my goals as designated on the first draft of my food & exercise recovery plan; however, I will increase my exercise time to 17 to 20 minutes on 3 days instead of 15 to 20 minutes (2) My new goal is to limit my eating at home to the kitchen 2 days next week._

2. What is my reward?

If I achieve my goal, I may: _buy myself a pair of earrings_

3. If I do not achieve my goal, I agree that I will not receive my reward.

Signed: _Jill Smith_

Date: _January 9_

4. I achieved my goal for this contract.

_____ Yes

_____ No, explain: _____

ABSTINENCE IN ACTION

Assignment

1. Fill out Food and Activity Records (on the following pages) each day for the next seven days.

2. Focus on achieving the food and exercise goals you have identified on your Food and Exercise Recovery Plan. Don't forget the new goal you have added to your Commitment Contract, and possibly an additional exercise goal.

3. Review the recommendations for preparing quick and nutritious meals at home that were identified in this chapter.

4. Wait seven days before reading Chapter Ten.

FOOD AND ACTIVITY RECORD

NAME: _____   _____ I EXERCISED FOR _____ CONSECUTIVE MINUTES

_____ I DID NOT EXERCISE

DATE	TIME	FOOD	AMOUNT	PLACE	HUNGER (0-5)	MOOD

ABSTINENCE IN ACTION

FOOD AND ACTIVITY RECORD

NAME: _____   _____ I EXERCISED FOR _____ CONSECUTIVE MINUTES

_____ I DID NOT EXERCISE

DATE	TIME	FOOD	AMOUNT	PLACE	HUNGER (0-5)	MOOD

FOOD AND ACTIVITY RECORD

NAME: _____   _____ I EXERCISED FOR _____ CONSECUTIVE MINUTES

_____ I DID NOT EXERCISE

DATE	TIME	FOOD	AMOUNT	PLACE	HUNGER (0-5)	MOOD

ABSTINENCE IN ACTION

FOOD AND ACTIVITY RECORD

NAME: _____   _____ I EXERCISED FOR _____ CONSECUTIVE MINUTES

_____ I DID NOT EXERCISE

DATE	TIME	FOOD	AMOUNT	PLACE	HUNGER (0-5)	MOOD

FOOD AND ACTIVITY RECORD

NAME: _____   _____ I EXERCISED FOR _____ CONSECUTIVE MINUTES

_____ I DID NOT EXERCISE

DATE	TIME	FOOD	AMOUNT	PLACE	HUNGER (0-5)	MOOD

ABSTINENCE IN ACTION

FOOD AND ACTIVITY RECORD

NAME: _____   _____ I EXERCISED FOR _____ CONSECUTIVE MINUTES

_____ I DID NOT EXERCISE

DATE	TIME	FOOD	AMOUNT	PLACE	HUNGER (0-5)	MOOD

FOOD AND ACTIVITY RECORD

NAME: _____   _____ I EXERCISED FOR _____ CONSECUTIVE MINUTES

_____ I DID NOT EXERCISE

DATE	TIME	FOOD	AMOUNT	PLACE	HUNGER (0-5)	MOOD

ABSTINENCE IN ACTION

Chapter 10

Carbohydrates, "Light" and "Low-Calorie" Foods

Did you find yourself eating on the run at home at some point last week? Did you choose to fix something quick at home, or did you decide to pick up something at a fast-food restaurant? Now that you've read Chapter Nine, you know that it is possible to prepare a quick, nutritious meal at home.

As we pointed out in the previous chapter, one convenient way to prepare a quick, nutritious home meal is to use frozen dinners (there are several varieties of "light" dinners now available at your supermarket). For a frozen dinner to be not just quick, but also healthy and nutritious, it should meet the criteria described on page 132.

Chapter Nine gave you the opportunity to evaluate two frozen dinner labels to see if the products met the quick and nutritious criteria. In addition to frozen dinners, we reviewed a variety of techniques and ideas for fixing quick, nutritious meals at home. For example, appliances such as the microwave can save a considerable amount of preparation and cooking time.

The advantages of cooking at home include the control you have over the fat, sodium, and nutrient content as well as the cost of the meals you prepare. But if you don't prepare meals with a concern for fat, sodium, cost, or nutritional quality, quick meals at home may no longer have an edge over restaurant meals.

In this chapter, we'll discuss carbohydrates, "light" and "low-calorie" foods. Let's get started with *carbohydrates*. What are they, and what role do they play in the weight management process?

Carbohydrates

Carbohydrates are best defined as the starch or sugar component of the foods we eat. Your body prefers carbohydrate as an energy source over fat and protein, which are the other two main sources of energy (calories) in food. The brain can only use carbohydrates to meet its energy needs.

Your body needs 100 grams of carbohydrates per day to keep it running smoothly. Each group of foods (listed below) will provide you with 100 grams of carbohydrate:

- 4 slices of bread
  2 pieces of fruit
  1 cup of cooked vegetables
  8 ounces of milk
- 1 ounce of cereal (ready to eat)
  1 bagel
  16 ounces of milk
  2 pieces of fruit
- 1 English muffin
  8 ounces of plain yogurt
  1 medium baked potato
  2 pieces of fruit
  ½ cup of cooked vegetables
- 2 cups of cooked spaghetti
  1 dinner roll
- 1 cup of cooked rice
  16 ounces of milk
  2 pieces of fruit
- 1 cup of beans (pinto, navy, kidney, et cetera)
  2 flour tortillas
  1 cup of cooked vegetables
  1 piece of fruit
  ½ cup of cooked rice

What will happen if you don't eat 100 grams of carbohydrate per day on a consistent basis? One or more of the following side effects will occur.

- Fatigue
- Loss of energy
- Dehydration
- Breakdown of body protein for energy.

Remember, carbohydrates are the only fuel source your brain can use. If you don't have enough carbohydrates your body breaks down protein so that carbohydrates can be made. This protein is taken from areas of your body, including your arm and leg muscles, heart, and kidneys. Unfortunately, your body can't break down body fat and change it into carbohydrates to energize your brain.

Thus, there are major drawbacks of low-carbohydrate diets, which can cause a loss of healthy muscle tissue — the tissue that burns up most of your calories for you. These diets can also be harmful to your health by breaking down the tissues in your heart and kidneys.

Simple Versus Complex Carbohydrates

All carbohydrates fall into two categories: simple and complex. Simple carbohydrates include foods such as cookies, candy, cakes, pies, and donuts. These foods require minimal digestion and provide calories but have limited nutritional value. Often, these foods are also high in fat.

Foods considered complex carbohydrates include breads, cereals, fruits, vegetables, pasta, dried beans, and peas. These foods generally are made of sugars and starch that have a more complicated structure, requiring more digestion than the sugars in simple carbohydrate foods.

Complex carbohydrate foods provide a great source of body energy and are low in fat. These foods also are good sources of vitamins and minerals. Fruits, vegetables, dried beans and peas, and whole grain products are good sources of natural fiber or bulk. Fiber or bulk gives food "filling power" without contributing many calories. For the compulsive eater, complex carbohydrate foods that are eaten raw, whole, unpeeled, and minimally cooked have two advantages over simple carbohydrate foods: (1) they take longer to eat and may offer greater satiety, and (2) they require more chewing (sometimes this chewing process can be satisfying in itself).

Light and Low-Calorie Foods

There is no legal definition for the term "light" or "lite." This means that if a food label tells you that the food inside is "light," the food may be moderate to low in fat, salt, sugar, cholesterol, or calories. On the other hand, the manufacturer may have arbitrarily decided to call the product "light."

The term "low-calorie" must meet specific guidelines. If a food label says "low-calorie," the product must not have any more than 40 calories per serving. Food labels indentifying the contents as being "reduced-calorie" must be at least one-third lower in calories per serving than a similar food that doesn't have reduced calories. Also, the "reduced-calorie" products must not be nutritionally inferior to the unmodified food.

If you have tried low-calorie or reduced-calorie foods, you probably found that some of these products satisfy the taste buds and some don't. It's important to use these foods only if you like how they taste and plan to use them indefinitely. If you use low- or reduced-calorie foods to manage your weight, but don't really like them, you may be setting yourself up for a binge. Most likely, the foods you choose to binge on will be ones that the "low-calorie" and "reduced-calorie" foods helped you to avoid.

Remember, it's better to use smaller quantities of foods you enjoy rather than substituting "low-calorie" foods you really don't like. This is an active step you can take in order to help control your compulsive eating and to help develop a realistic relationship with food.

Commitment Contract Review

Review your Food and Activity Records from the past week to determine whether or not your Food and Exercise Recovery Plan is working and realistic for you. If you fulfilled your goals, follow through with the reward you identified on your Commitment Contract. Be sure to revise your goals if you are having difficulty meeting them.

Commitment Contract: Upcoming Week

Use the Commitment Contract in Table XXVI on the next page to design your goals for the upcoming week. Continue to work on your Food and Exercise Recovery Plan and the additional goal you chose last week. If you haven't increased your exercise commitment, give serious consideration to this effort. Refer to Table XXVII on page 152 for an example of how to complete this week's contract.

TABLE XXVI
COMMITMENT CONTRACT

Name: _____

Period of Contract: From _____ to _____

1. What is my goal?

My goal is: _____

_____

_____

_____

_____

2. What is my reward?

If I achieve my goal, I may: _____

_____

_____

3. If I do not achieve my goal, I agree that I will not receive my reward.

Signed: _____

Date: _____

4. I achieved my goal for this contract.

_____ Yes

_____ No, explain: _____

_____

_____

TABLE XXVII
SAMPLE COMMITMENT CONTRACT

Name: _Jill Smith_

Period of Contract: From _January 16_ to _January 23_

1. What is my goal?

My goal is: _(1) To continue following my goals as designated on the first draft of my food and exercise recovery plan. I will keep my exercise at the increased time of 17 to 20 minutes on 3 days. (2) I will continue to limit my eating at home to the kitchen 2 days next week._

2. What is my reward?

If I achieve my goal, I may: _have the bathroom to myself for 30 minutes so I can enjoy a relaxing bubble bath._

3. If I do not achieve my goal, I agree that I will not receive my reward.

Signed: _Jill Smith_

Date: _January 16_

4. I achieved my goal for this contract.

_____ Yes

_____ No, explain: _____

_____

_____

Assignment

1. Fill out the Food and Activity Records (on the following pages) each day for the next seven days.

2. Focus on achieving the food and exercise goals you have identified on your Food and Exercise Recovery Plan. Don't forget about the new goal you added to your Commitment Contract last week. Did you update your exercise commitment?

3. Take time to look at some food labels that are identified as "low-calorie" or "reduced-calorie" and "light." Ask yourself, after evaluating the labels, whether the products are really saving you that much in the way of fat or calories.

4. Wait seven days before reading Chapter Eleven.

FOOD AND ACTIVITY RECORD

NAME: _____   _____ I EXERCISED FOR _____ CONSECUTIVE MINUTES

_____ I DID NOT EXERCISE

DATE	TIME	FOOD	AMOUNT	PLACE	HUNGER (0-5)	MOOD

ABSTINENCE IN ACTION

FOOD AND ACTIVITY RECORD

NAME: _____   _____ I EXERCISED FOR _____ CONSECUTIVE MINUTES

_____ I DID NOT EXERCISE

DATE	TIME	FOOD	AMOUNT	PLACE	HUNGER (0-5)	MOOD

FOOD AND ACTIVITY RECORD

NAME: _____   _____ I EXERCISED FOR _____ CONSECUTIVE MINUTES

_____ I DID NOT EXERCISE

DATE	TIME	FOOD	AMOUNT	PLACE	HUNGER (0-5)	MOOD

ABSTINENCE IN ACTION

FOOD AND ACTIVITY RECORD

NAME: _____   _____ I EXERCISED FOR _____ CONSECUTIVE MINUTES
_____ I DID NOT EXERCISE

DATE	TIME	FOOD	AMOUNT	PLACE	HUNGER (0-5)	MOOD

FOOD AND ACTIVITY RECORD

NAME: _____   _____ I EXERCISED FOR _____ CONSECUTIVE MINUTES

_____ I DID NOT EXERCISE

DATE	TIME	FOOD	AMOUNT	PLACE	HUNGER (0-5)	MOOD

FOOD AND ACTIVITY RECORD

NAME: _____   _____ I EXERCISED FOR _____ CONSECUTIVE MINUTES

_____ I DID NOT EXERCISE

DATE	TIME	FOOD	AMOUNT	PLACE	HUNGER (0-5)	MOOD

FOOD AND ACTIVITY RECORD

NAME: _____   _____ I EXERCISED FOR _____ CONSECUTIVE MINUTES

_____ I DID NOT EXERCISE

DATE	TIME	FOOD	AMOUNT	PLACE	HUNGER (0-5)	MOOD

ABSTINENCE IN ACTION

Chapter 11

Putting It All Together: Part II

Last week in Chapter Ten you were given information about the importance of including carbohydrates in your Food and Exercise Recovery Plan. The recommended level of carbohydrate essential to keeping your brain and body running smoothly is 100 grams per day. This gram figure was translated into practical food examples.

You learned the difference between simple and complex carbohydrates. In addition, the advantages of using complex carbohydrates versus simple carbohydrates, especially as part of a weight management effort, were identified.

Finally, you were presented with guidelines on how to decipher the following terms when they appear on food labels: "light," "lite," "low-calorie," and "reduced-calorie."

Now it's time to congratulate yourself. You have progressed to the eleventh chapter of this program. Although this is almost the final chapter of this book, it should not be viewed as part of the final chapter in your recovery. It's important to remind yourself that recovery is an ongoing process, a lifetime commitment.

This chapter is designed to help you assess how your behavior has changed regarding three important components of your recovery: (1) your relationship with food, (2) your eating behaviors, and (3) your exercise habits. You will be using the following methods to do your assessment: (1) The Compulsive Eater's Behavior Inventory, (2) your physical measurements, and (3) a combined review of your Personal Food and Exercise Recovery Plan and your Commitment Contracts.

The Compulsive Eater's Behavior Inventory is an effective way to help you measure your behavior changes because you can compare your scores and answers on the inventory in this chapter to the scores and answers in the same inventory you completed during the first week of this program. In order to get the best reflection of your progress toward strengthening your recovery from compulsive eating, do not review your answers and scores on your first inventory until after you've finished this chapter's inventory.

Please take ten to fifteen minutes to complete the following inventory. Place an "X" in the column that most accurately represents your response to the statements. **Note:** "x/week" means "times per week." For example: 2 to 3 x/week would read 2 to 3 times per week.

Score your behavior inventory when you have completely finished. Please do not score it as you fill it out.

THE COMPULSIVE EATER'S BEHAVIOR INVENTORY

I. MEAL TIMING/FREQUENCY

1. I eat my first meal before noon.

_____	Never or rarely	0
_____	2 to 3 x/week	1
_____	4 to 6 x/week	2
_____	Every day	3

2. I eat after 7:00 P.M.

_____	Never or rarely	3
_____	2 to 3 x/week	2
_____	4 to 6 x/week	1
_____	Every day	0

THE COMPULSIVE EATER'S BEHAVIOR INVENTORY (Continued)

3. I eat less than three times a day.

_____	Never or rarely	3
_____	2 to 3 x/week	2
_____	4 to 6 x/week	1
_____	Every day	0

4. I eat more than five times a day.

_____	Never or rarely	3
_____	2 to 3 x/week	2
_____	4 to 6 x/week	1
_____	Every day	0

Total _____

II. BINGE FOODS

1. I eat foods high in sugar: pop, cakes, sweetened cereals.

_____	Never or rarely	0
_____	4 or more x/day	1
_____	2 to 3 x/day	2
_____	1 x/day	3
_____	3 to 6 x/week	4

2. I eat foods high in fat: lunch meat, salad dressing, hot dogs, fried foods.

_____	Never or rarely	0
_____	4 or more x/day	1
_____	2 to 3 x/day	2
_____	1 x/day	3
_____	3 to 6 x/week	4

3. I eat at fast-food restaurants.

_____	Never or rarely	0
_____	4 or more x/day	1
_____	2 to 3 x/day	2
_____	1 x/day	3
_____	3 to 6 x/week	4

4. I eat snack foods: chips, pretzels, candy, and ice cream.

   _____ Never or rarely   0

   _____ 4 or more x/day   1

   _____ 2 to 3 x/day   2

   _____ 1 x/day   3

   _____ 3 to 6 x/week   4

Total _____

III. BINGING

1. I pre-plan what foods I will eat.

   _____ Never or rarely   0

   _____ 2 to 3 x/week   1

   _____ 4 to 6 x/week   2

   _____ Every day   3

2. I count the calories in the foods I eat.

   _____ Never or rarely   3

   _____ 2 to 3 x/week   2

   _____ 4 to 6 x/week   1

   _____ Every day   0

3. I weigh myself.

   _____ Never or rarely   3

   _____ 2 to 3 x/week   2

   _____ 4 to 6 x/week   1

   _____ Every day   0

4. I follow a diet to help me lose weight.

   _____ Never   3

   _____ 2 to 3 x/week   2

   _____ 4 to 6 x/week   1

   _____ Every day   0

Total _____

THE COMPULSIVE EATER'S BEHAVIOR INVENTORY (Continued)

IV. ENVIRONMENT/FEELINGS

A. PLACE

1. I eat or drink in the car.

_____ Never or rarely	3
_____ 2 to 4 x/week	2
_____ 1 x/day	1
_____ 2 or more x/day	0

2. I eat or drink while standing at the refrigerator.

_____ Never or rarely	3
_____ 2 to 4 x/week	2
_____ 1 x/day	1
_____ 2 or more x/day	0

3. I eat while watching TV

_____ Never or rarely	3
_____ 2 to 4 x/week	2
_____ 1 x/day	1
_____ 2 or more x/day	0

4. I limit my eating to only one room in the house. For example, the kitchen.

_____ Never or rarely	0
_____ 2 to 4 x/week	1
_____ 1 x/day	2
_____ 2 or more x/day	3

Total _____

B. HUNGER LEVEL

1. I eat when I feel physically hungry.

_____ Never or rarely   0
_____ 2 to 4 x/week   1
_____ 1 x/day   2
_____ 2 or more x/day   3

2. I eat even when I am not very hungry.

_____ Never or rarely   3
_____ 2 to 4 x/week   2
_____ 1 x/day   1
_____ 2 or more x/day   0

3. I eat because it is time to eat (for example, it's noon and that means lunch).

_____ Never or rarely   3
_____ 2 to 4 x/week   2
_____ 1 x/day   1
_____ 2 or more x/day   0

4. I skip breakfast because I'm not hungry in the morning.

_____ Never or rarely   3
_____ 2 to 3 x/week   2
_____ 4 to 6 x/week   1
_____ Every day   0

5. I know when I'm physically hungry.

_____ Never or rarely   0
_____ 2 to 4 x/week   1
_____ 1 x/day   2
_____ 2 or more x/day   3

Total _____

C MOOD

1. I eat when I am anxious or nervous.

	Never or rarely	3
_____	2 to 3 x/week	2
_____	4 to 6 x/week	1
_____	Every day	0

2. I eat when I am bored.

	Never or rarely	3
_____	2 to 3 x/week	2
_____	4 to 6 x/week	1
_____	Every day	0

3. I eat to relax.

	Never or rarely	3
_____	2 to 3 x/week	2
_____	4 to 6 x/week	1
_____	Every day	0

4. I eat in response to moods.

	Never or rarely	3
_____	2 to 3 x/week	2
_____	4 to 6 x/week	1
_____	Every day	0

Total _____

THE COMPULSIVE EATER'S BEHAVIOR INVENTORY (Continued)

V. PORTION SIZES

1. I eat serving sizes of meat, fish, or chicken at one meal that are four or more ounces.

   _____ Never or rarely   3
   _____ 2 to 4 x/week   2
   _____ 1 x/day   1
   _____ 2 or more x/day   0

2. I eat serving sizes of meat, fish, or chicken at one meal that are two to three ounces.

   _____ Never or rarely   0
   _____ 2 to 4 x/week   1
   _____ 1 x/day   2
   _____ 2 or more x/day   3

3. I eat serving sizes of starch (spaghetti, noodles, rice) at one meal in ½ cup quantities or greater.

   _____ Never or rarely   0
   _____ 2 to 4 x/week   1
   _____ 1 x/day   2
   _____ 2 or more x/day   3

4. I consume serving sizes of milk or yogurt at one meal that are in 1 cup (8 oz.) quantities.

   _____ Never or rarely   0
   _____ 2 to 4 x/week   1
   _____ 1 x/day   2
   _____ 2 or more x/day   3

5. I eat serving sizes of vegetables at one meal in ½ cup quantities or greater.

   _____ Never or rarely   0
   _____ 2 to 3 x/week   1
   _____ 1 x/day   2
   _____ 2 or more x/day   3

Total _____

THE COMPULSIVE EATER'S BEHAVIOR INVENTORY (Continued)

VI. EXERCISE/ACTIVITY

1. I do some type of exercise (for example, walking, biking, swimming) for 20 to 30 consecutive minutes.

   _____ Never or rarely   0
   _____ 2 to 3 x/week   1
   _____ 4 to 6 x/week   2
   _____ Every day   3

2. I monitor my heart rate when I exercise.

   _____ Never or rarely   0
   _____ 2 to 3 x/week   1
   _____ 4 to 6 x/week   2
   _____ Every day   3

3. I do some type of exercise such as gardening, painting, housework, chasing after kids.

   _____ Never or rarely   0
   _____ 2 to 3 x/week   1
   _____ 4 to 6 x/week   2
   _____ Every day   3

4. I make a special effort to include exercise in my daily routine (for example, using stairs instead of elevators, or parking the car far from store entrances).

   _____ Never or rarely   0
   _____ 2 to 3 x/week   1
   _____ 4 to 6 x/week   2
   _____ Every day   3

5. I exercise for 45 minutes or longer daily, 5 or more times per week, and feel guilty if I am unable to fit one of these exercise sessions into my schedule.

   _____ Never or rarely   3
   _____ 2 to 3 x/week   2
   _____ 4 to 6 x/week   1
   _____ Every day   0

Total _____

Go back to each category and circle the number 0, 1, 2, 3, or 4 next to each answer you've checked. For each group of questions, add up your scores and enter on the *Total* line.

After you score your inventory, compare your answers and scores for each category against those from the completed inventory in Chapter One. Those categories in which you received higher scores this time are ones in which your relationship with food, your eating behaviors, and your exercise habits have improved. Categories in which your scores are low at this time need work and should be included in your Personal Food and Exercise Recovery Plan.

Physical measurements are a visual way of evaluating your progress. It's important for consistency that the same person who did your body measurements during week one do them now. Record the measurements in the appropriate spaces in Table VI (Body Part Measurements) on page 30 and calculate the differences between the two sets of measurements.

Changes in weight or physical measurements may not be dramatic, since nine weeks is a short time. The amount of weight loss may vary from zero to sixteen pounds. Some physical measurements may have decreased as much as an inch. It's important to recognize that the amount of change seen in physical measurements will be in proportion to the amount of time you devoted to your Commitment Contracts and your food and exercise plan. If you're starting to feel comfortable with your recovery plan, a weight gain of zero or stable physical measurements can be considered a major accomplishment.

◆ ◆ ◆

So far you've used the Compulsive Eater's Behavior Inventory and your physical measurements to analyze your progress. We recommend that you also review your Commitment Contracts to determine whether your current Personal Food and Exercise Recovery Plan is realistic. The Commitment Contract is your direct link to incorporating this program's Abstinence in Action Recovery Plan into your food and exercise plan.

Take time now to look over your Commitment Contracts. On how many contracts did you meet both your food and exercise goals? When you didn't meet your goals, what explanation did you give on your contract? Were your goals realistic? Did you adjust goals that you didn't meet so that they were more realistic the next week? Have you made this program and your recovery plan a major priority? Did you focus on the most difficult aspects of your relationship with food and your food behaviors? Doing this could set you up for failure.

If you were successful on your Commitment Contracts this means your goals are realistic and that your recovery plan is working.

You have now completed the assessment of your progress. You should have a good idea of where you currently stand in recovery from compulsive eating. Now, you need to decide how to further your recovery. The best way to do this is to use the information you obtained from your assessment in this chapter to design a new or updated version of your Personal Food and Exercise Recovery Plan. Take time now to use Table XXVIII on the following pages for this purpose. If you need help with this process, review the instructions and guidelines presented in Chapter Seven where you developed the first draft of your Personal Food and Exercise Recovery Plan.

TABLE XXVIII
MY PERSONAL FOOD AND
EXERCISE RECOVERY PLAN

I. FOOD RELATIONSHIPS AND BEHAVIORS

1. Meal Timing/Frequency

My goal is to: _____

_____

_____

_____

2. Binge Foods (sweets and foods high in fat)

My goal is to: _____

_____

_____

_____

3. Binging

My goal is to: _____

_____

_____

_____

4. Environment and Feelings

My goal is to: _____

_____

_____

_____

ABSTINENCE IN ACTION

TABLE XXVIII
MY PERSONAL FOOD AND
EXERCISE RECOVERY PLAN (Continued)

II. FOOD STRATEGY GUIDELINE

My goal is to: _____

_____

_____

_____

Meal #1 (Time: _____)

Protein _____

Dairy _____

Grain
Bread/Starch _____

Fruit/Vegetable _____

Beverage _____

Other/Fats _____

Meal #2 (Time: _____)

Protein _____

Dairy _____

Grain
Bread/Starch _____

Fruit/Vegetable _____

Beverage _____

Other/Fats _____

TABLE XXVIII
MY PERSONAL FOOD AND
EXERCISE RECOVERY PLAN (Continued)

Meal #3 (Time: _____)

Protein _____

Dairy _____

Grain
Bread/Starch _____

Fruit/Vegetable _____

Beverage _____

Other/Fats _____

III. EXERCISE/ACTIVITY

My goal is to: _____

_____

_____

_____

Brief Review

The overall objective of this program was threefold:

- To educate you regarding basic nutrition and food facts.
- To guide you through structured activities so that you would be able to integrate this information into your recovery program.
- To help you develop a sound, flexible food and exercise plan that would help strengthen your recovery from compulsive eating.

If you spent time and effort in your food and activity records, your weekly Commitment Contracts, and the information and activities presented throughout this book, you have probably strengthened your recovery from compulsive eating. The Personal Food and Exercise Recovery Plan that you designed in this chapter will continue to further your recovery from compulsive eating as long as you keep updating it to accommodate your needs and goals.

Chapter 12

Relapse

Relapse among compulsive eaters is very common. Many people think that relapse begins with the first binge or the use of a diet plan, diet pill, or diet food. But relapse is a progressive process that leads to a destructive relationship with food. Relapse is an indication that compulsive eaters need to reflect on the quality of their recovery program, abstinence concept, food and exercise plan, and their involvement in the Twelve Steps and support group work.

Relapse is a process that occurs *within* the individual; it manifests itself in a progressive style of behaving that reactivates the symptoms of the disease.

Symptoms of Relapse for the Compulsive Eater

Relapse for compulsive eaters usually occurs in two stages. Stage one is the actual binge behavior as a final response to a series of stressful situations. Stage two occurs even though the compulsive eater decides not to binge any further, but instead chooses to regain control by some form of rigid dieting and exercising.

Abstaining from dieting is a major form of relapse prevention for compulsive eaters. The dieting behavior affects the metabolism which consequently affects weight gain. Rather than a return to dieting, if compulsive eaters return to their food and exercise plan after a binge episode, they will be making great strides in strengthening their recovery program in two important ways.

First, they build confidence in themselves to rely on their resources to manage their eating, rather than depending on rigid external controls.

Secondly, their metabolism is not ravaged by excessive food restriction or the use of a single food group.

Warning Signs

We have found that the following are some of the warning signs of relapse for many compulsive eaters.

1. *They are unable to express anger constructively or to be assertive.*

This is perhaps the most common reason compulsive eaters give for returning to binge eating. They feel anger or feel bad about being angry and they end up repressing the anger or doing or saying something they really don't mean or feel. This stirs up their feelings of powerlessness.

2. *They are unable to manage uncomfortable feelings such as anxiety or depression.*

Some compulsive eaters have difficulty when they feel any strong emotion, particularly a negative one. They may interpret this as a sign of weakness. They believe that strong, independent people are always in control and aren't overwhelmed by feelings.

3. *Dissatisfaction with their lives.*

Most compulsive eaters begin to feel that life would be so much better if they were thin. People would like them better. They would like themselves better. Life would be more fun. The "if only I were thinner" syndrome again supports the belief that thin equals control, independence, and strength.

4. *They are feeling powerless.*

The "if only I were thinner" syndrome contributes to feelings of powerlessness. A lot of compulsive eaters look outside of themselves to be rescued from their problems. They have difficulty taking responsibility for their actions and decisions.

5. *They have overwhelming feelings of loneliness and of not belonging.*

A major signal that a relapse is on the way is when compulsive eaters isolate themselves. They start withdrawing from people and refuse to participate in group activities. They retreat more and more into their loneliness and feeling that there is no one who really cares about them.

6. *Relapse might occur when they are disappointed or hurt by a loved one.*

For a number of reasons, some compulsive eaters depend a great deal on their relationships to provide them with security, comfort, and acceptance. In exchange, they are willing to do almost anything to preserve the relationship or to make the other person happy. They might blame themselves if a loved one disappoints them. *There must be something wrong with me* is a common feeling. Consequently, they have difficulty in their relationships because they have unrealistic expectations of themselves and of the people with whom they are involved.

These feelings, attitudes, and beliefs can culminate in a binge episode. It may start with a small deviation from the food and exercise plan or it can be a full-blown binge.

What to Do

The first and most important step is to know your specific warning signs of a potential relapse.

We encourage our patients to develop a checklist of their warning signs and then to assess daily their progress in each area. This takes about ten minutes. We encourage them to do the assessment in the evening along with a review of their food and activity records.

Some signs our patients have include:

- I did not express my anger today.
- I was people pleasing today.
- My self-talk was negative today.
- I expected myself to be perfect today.
- I retreated into myself today.
- I was not as honest as I could have been today with someone.
- I agreed to do something that I did not really want to do.

Make a list of your own and do a daily assessment. If you're checking a lot of warning symptoms, you may be in the process of relapse. Check your food and activity records and re-evaluate your Personal Food and Exercise Plan. Use your Compulsive Eater's Behavior Inventory and study your Abstinence in Action Recovery Plan. These tools will help. Finally, we hope that this book has helped and will continue to help to strengthen your abstinence concept and your ability to develop a flexible food and exercise plan.

Suggested Reading

Bailey, Covert. *Fit or Fat?* Boston: Houghton Mifflin Co., 1977.

Brody, Jane. *Jane Brody's Good Food Book: Living the High Carbohydrate Way.* New York: W. W. Norton, 1985.

Brody, Jane. *Jane Brody's Nutrition Book.* New York: W. W. Norton, 1981.

Cumming, Candy and Vicky Newman. *Eaters Guide: Nutrition Basics for Busy People.* Englewood Cliffs, N.J.: Prentice Hall, Inc., 1981.

Hollis, Judi. *Fat Is a Family Affair.* Center City, Minn.: Hazelden Educational Materials, 1985.

Jacobson, Michael and Sarah Fritschner. *The Fast Food Nutrition Guide: What's Good, What's Bad, and How to Tell the Difference.* New York: Workman Publishing Co., 1986.

Jordan, Henry A., Leonard S. Levitz, and Gordon M. Kimbrell. *Eating Is Okay: A Radical Approach to Weight Loss.* New York: Signet, 1976.

Listen to the Hunger. Center City, Minn.: Hazelden Educational Materials, 1987.

Methven, Barbara. *Microwaving on a Diet.* Minnetonka, Minn.: Cy DeCosse, Inc., 1981.

Mirkin, Gabe and Laura Foreman. *Getting Thin.* Boston: Little, Brown, and Co., 1983.

Remington, Dennis. *How to Lower Your Fat Thermostat.* Provo, Utah: Vitality House International, Inc., 1983.

Schwartz, Bob. *Diets Don't Work.* Las Vegas: Breakthru Publishing, 1982.

INDEX

A

Abstinence: concept of, 2, 4; Model for compulsive eaters, 5-6
Abstinence in Action Recovery Plan, 15-17, 97
Aerobic exercises, 41
American Heart Association, 88

B

Behavior change, in recovery, 161-62
Binging, 5, 16
Body composition, 40-41

C

Carbohydrates: definition of, 148; requirements, 148-49; types of, 149
Commitment Contracts, 24-26, 45-48, 66-68, 84-86, 119-21, 136-38, 150-52
Complex carbohydrates, 149
Compulsive Eater's Behavior Inventory, The, 7-15, 162-69
Compulsive eating: as a disease, 1-2, 4; control issue in, 1, 3; treatment of, 2. *See also* Abstinence
Conscious eating, 16-17
Control, issue of, in compulsive eating, 1, 3
Conversion check test, 42
Culture, and dieting, 3-4

D

Denial, 1, 3
Dieting, 2-4

E

Eating: at fast food restaurants, 77-79; at home, 131-36; at regular restaurants, 80-83
Eating disorders, 3
Eating Disorders Recovery Center, 2
Emotional abstinence, 5
Exercise: benefits of, 39-40; body composition and, 40-41; in recovery plan, 19; types of, 41

F

Fast food eating, 77-79
Fast Food Restaurant Corporate Headquarters Addresses, 88
Fat: benefits of, 57-60; consumption of, 113; content identification, 118-19; content in fast foods, 77-79; foods high in, 15-16, 60-63
Fat Finding Activity, 114-117
Fat reduction: benefits, 57-60, 113-14; Fat Finding Activity, 114-17; Trimming Fat and Refined Sugar, 63-65
Fat weight, 40-41
Food, relationship to, in recovery, 5
Food and Activity Records, 21-23, 32-28, 49-55, 70-76, 89-95, 105-11, 123-29, 140-46, 154-60
Food and exercise plan, overview, 6
Food labels, 118-19
Food Strategy Guideline, 18
Frozen Dinner Evaluation, 134-35
Frozen dinners, 131-32

G

Getting To Know Your Fat Worksheet, 61

L

Light foods, 149
Low-calorie foods, 149-50
Low-carbohydrate diets, 148-49

M

Meal planning, 15-16, 131
Muscle weight, 40-41

O

Overeaters Anonymous, 4

P

Personal Food and Exercise Plan, 97-104, 171-74
Physical abstinence, 5
Physical measurements, 29-30, 170
Portion sizes, 17-19
Professional therapy, 4
Pulse rate, 44
Purging, 3

R

Recovery program: overview of, 4-6; review of, 175
Reduced-calorie foods, 150
Relapse, 177-79
Restaurant dining, 80-83

S

Simple carbohydrates, 149. *See also* Sugar
Spiritual abstinence, 5
Stress, and compulsive eating, 1
Sugar, foods high in, 15-16, 63-65

T

The Compulsive Eater's Behavior Inventory, 7-15, 162-69
Trimming Fat and Refined Sugar, 63-65

W

Weight loss, and dieting, 3
Working heart rate, 42-43